Team Policing

SEVEN CASE STUDIES

Principal Authors
Lawrence W. Sherman
Catherine H. Milton
Thomas V. Kelly

Contributing Authors
Thomas F. McBride
Susan Michaelson
Robert Wasserman

Foreword by
James Q. Wilson

Police Foundation
1015 Eighteenth Street, N.W.
Washington, D.C. 20036

Police Foundation
1015 Eighteenth Street, N.W.
Washington, D.C. 20036

Lawrence W. Sherman is a graduate student of sociology at Yale University and a consultant to the Police Foundation. He formerly served in the Inspectional Services Bureau and the Police Commissioner's Office, New York City Police Department, and has also been a consultant to the Kansas City, Missouri Police Department. He received the B.A. from Denison University and the M.A. from the University of Chicago, both in 1970, and the Diploma in Criminology from Cambridge University in 1973.

Catherine H. Milton is an Assistant Director of the Police Foundation. She previously served on the staffs of the International Association of Chiefs of Police and the President's Commission on Student Unrest, and worked as a reporter for *The Boston Globe.* Author of several publications including *Women in Policing,* she graduated from Mount Holyoke College in 1964.

Thomas V. Kelly is a free-lance writer, who formerly served as Director of National Affairs for VISTA. He is a frequent contributor to the *Washingtonian* magazine.

Acknowledgements

Over the months required to complete this study, we have incurred many debts to many people. In 1971, former Police Commissioner Patrick V. Murphy gave Lawrence Sherman the opportunity to monitor New York's embryo Neighborhood Team Policing program, and that led to further research. Charles H. Rogovin, former President of the Police Foundation, approved Foundation support of the initial research in other cities. The police and municipal administrators in each of the seven case study cities were extremely cooperative with the research: former Dayton Police Director Robert M. Igleburger, Detroit Police Commissioner John F. Nichols, Syracuse Police Chief Thomas Sardino, Los Angeles Police Chief Edward M. Davis, Holyoke Mayor William Taupier, Richmond Police Chief Lourn Phelps, and the present New York City Police Commissioner Donald Cawley.

Many others provided useful comments on many drafts, including James Elliott, Mark Furstenberg, Peter Bloch, John Angell, Raymond Galvin, Michael Gardner, Beryl Radin, Elizabeth Howe, Ronald Breedlove and Sophy Burnham. Joseph H. Lewis, Police Foundation Director of Evaluation, contributed to the chapter on evaluations. Though all these deserve many thanks, most deserving of thanks are the team policing officers who are dedicated to improving the quality of police service in America.

Contents

Foreword by James Q. Wilson ix

Introduction xiii

Chapter I. Elements of Team Policing 1

Chapter II. Case Studies 9

    Dayton 11

    Detroit 23

    New York City 28

    Syracuse 34

    Holyoke 39

    Los Angeles 45

    Richmond 54

Chapter III. Preparation for Team Policing:

    Goals, Plans and Training 59

Chapter IV. Team Policing on the Street 71

Chapter V. Obstacles to Team Policing 89

Chapter VI. Evaluations 97

Chapter VII. Summary and Conclusions 105

Foreword

The police administrator faces a dilemma. He is aware that corruption and the abuse of authority are constant dangers on his force, that rioting and collective violence have occurred before in his city and may occur again, and that people are frightened and want visible evidence of a massive police presence that will reduce crime. He also knows that, however much the city council may complain of rising crime rates, it is also concerned about rising tax rates and thus wants the police department run as economically as possible. For all these reasons, the police administrator is tempted to organize and operate his department along tight, quasi-military lines with strict supervision of patrol officers, a strong command structure that can deploy effectively large numbers of police in emergency situations, powerful and mobile tactical forces that can saturate areas experiencing high crime rates, and close controls over costs, scheduling, assignments, and discipline.

But he also is aware that his patrol officers exercise great discretion and thus can never be fully supervised, that much of their time is spent on noncriminal matters, that some parts of the community fear and distrust the police while other parts want closer contact with them, that massive displays of police power can sometimes exacerbate tense situations, and that quasi-military discipline can lower the morale and perhaps the effectiveness of many officers. For these reasons, he is tempted to organize his department along highly decentralized lines, with considerable discretionary authority given to patrol officers and their sergeants, great attention given to the resolution of community disputes and the provision of social services, and little use of tactical forces.

There are two reasons why the administrator regards this choice as posing a dilemma: First, he has very little evidence, other than his own hunches and the lore of his craft, which of these two models of policing is most likely to succeed, or even what "success" means. Second, being an experienced officer, he is aware that both theories of policing are correct in some measure, and thus gains from wholly adopting one will create costs from having foregone the other. For example, the military model may result in a prompt response to radio calls, but since answering all calls promptly means spending as little time as possible on any given call, an officer cannot learn much or be of much help to a citizen who calls. On the other hand, the service model will enable the officer to devote time and expertise to helping a citizen who calls but at the cost of postponing answering other calls or referring them to officers who are not as familiar with the area.

Even if the administrator could be clear in his own mind as to what he wants, he faces two important constraints on his freedom of action, one internal to the department and the other external to it. His officers, in all likelihood, will be accustomed to one way of doing things and they will see any effort to change that as a threat, not only to their habits and expectations, but to their promotion prospects, work schedules, and authority. Community groups, on the other hand, will be divided as to what they want: some neighborhoods may welcome tough, vigorous policing as a way of keeping the streets safe and the "kids in their place," while others may prefer a police force that is closely integrated with the community and perhaps even subject to its control. Indeed, it is likely that any given community will want both things at once—be tough and concerned, visible and invisible, enforcement-oriented and service-oriented.

Team policing should be seen as an effort, one of many possible, to test these competing views and form a realistic and objective assessment of what kinds of police deployment produce what results under which circumstances. This is not to say that it is merely an experiment, designed to satisfy curiosity or gather data. Rather, it is a police strategy—or more accurately, a collection of somewhat similar police strategies—which some police administrators believe may be a partial solution to the dilemma they face. In theory it combines the advantages of a substantial police presence in a neighborhood, deployed to put the maximum number of officers on the street during times of greatest need and supervised so as to encourage the maximum use of information about the area and its citizens, with the advantages of a police style devoted to servicing complaints, helping citizens, and establishing good relations.

But so far it is only a theory. It is still too early to tell whether this strategy will realize the expectations of its creators. In presenting the case studies and analysis that follows, the Police Foundation is not suggesting that team policing, in any of its many variants, is *the* answer to the police dilemma, or even that we are now in a position to know what an answer is. We believe that it is a promising approach but one that is still somewhat vague in conception, weak in execution, and uncertain in results. In time, we hope that by carefully designing and testing several different police strategies, various police departments will obtain information that can be widely disseminated as to the circumstances under which one police strategy, or some combination of strategies, produces gains in crime control, citizen service, and community support. The Police Foundation is engaged in helping departments try approaches they have formulated to see what works and what does not.

It is this approach—testing and evaluating—rather than the substantive content of any given strategy that is important. Not every city, or every part of any city, may be well served by a single police strategy. Yet in the past, our police strategies were picked, or rather they emerged out of historical forces, without much systematic reflection as to how well they might help control crime, or help citizens. Indeed, until recently we did not think in terms of a police "strategy" or "style" that could be deliberately chosen. We tended instead to accept either what existed as historically foreordained or what was proposed by "leading authorities" as unquestionably correct. At one time our cities were policed by watchmen who not only walked a beat, but who managed it and the people on it with a minimum of supervision and relatively few arrests. Some cities still display the watchman style. In reaction to this, advocates of centralized control, close supervision, and maximum enforcement arose, whose textbooks and personal example created a new era of policing that was called "professionalism." Now some of the doctrines of that school are being questioned by those who believe that professionalism separated the police from the community and over-emphasized writing tickets and making arrests.

It is not the purpose of this publication to offer any new dogma to replace the dogmas of yesterday. It is rather to show how some cities went about the task of finding new solutions to the police dilemma and to offer some preliminary findings about what will happen as a result. In future publications, the Foundation will offer more systematic evidence on additional projects that are now underway.

JAMES Q. WILSON

Shattuck Professor of Government
Harvard University
Vice Chairman, Police Foundation

Introduction

The urban unrest of the 1960's made it clear that there was much dissatisfaction with government in general and the police in particular. The kind of policing done in many communities was clearly not the kind of policing those communities wanted. Many police administrators ignored the basic issue of community differences, asking only for more money, men, and equipment. But some police administrators met the crisis by reorganizing their departments to make them more responsive to the range of community needs in their cities.

Among the responses were a number of small pilot projects known by the general label of "team policing." Team policing meant something different in each city, but generally it has been an attempt to strike a new balance between the presumed efficiency needs of police centralization and community needs for police decentralization in order to be more responsive to citizens.

The term "team policing" originated in Aberdeen, Scotland immediately after World War II. The Aberdeen project began as an effort to counteract the low morale and boredom of single officers patrolling quiet streets. It allocated teams of five and ten men on foot and in cars to cover the city. The patrols were distributed according to concentration of crimes and calls for service, with the teams moved to different parts of the city as the workload demanded. The monotony and loneliness of the patrolmen were thus relieved.

A second form of team policing, called "Unit Beat Policing," appeared in the town of Accrington in the County of Coventry, England, in 1966. Its stated purpose was to overcome a shortage of manpower by effectively utilizing the existing limited resources. Under the Coventry Unit Beat Policing system, constables were organized into teams which remained in one specific area. Although the constables working in the same area did not patrol as a team, they all fed information about their area to a central collator who was responsible for the exchange of knowledge about that area. By maximizing coordination and the exchange of information through the collator, fewer men could cover a wider territory than they had previously been able to.

The Aberdeen system was abandoned in 1963 but had already been tried in Tucson, Arizona and a number of other small American cities. The Coventry form of team policing is still in practice and has been expanded to other police forces in England; it is the form most prevalent in the United States and generally known as "neighborhood team policing." A third variant combines aspects of both the Aberdeen (manpower allocated according to workload) and Coventry (neighborhood-based) systems and was instituted in Richmond, California in 1968.

In 1967, the President's Commission on Law Enforcement and the Administration of Justice recommended the following:

> Police departments should commence experimentation with a team policing concept that envisions those officers with patrol and investigative duties combining under unified command with flexible assignments to deal with the crime problem in a defined sector.

By 1973 a number of American cities had experimented with team policing in one way or another. In theory, the patrol force is reorganized to include one or more quasi-autonomous teams, with a joint purpose of improving police services to the community and increasing job satisfaction of the patrol officers. Usually the team is based in a particular neighborhood. Each team has responsibility for police services in its neighborhood and is intended to work as a unit in close contact with the community to prevent crime and maintain order. In practice, team policing has not always been able to accomplish these goals, although it seems to have come very close in some cities. In others, team policing has become a label, a public relations device. In still others, there has been a measure of achievement, but it has been less than was anticipated by those who launched the project.

This study was undertaken to examine the team policing experience on a case-by-case basis and to get some preliminary indications of why team policing has worked well in some places and less well in others. Seven cities were chosen:

- two small cities—Holyoke, Massachusetts and Richmond, California
- two middle-sized cities—Dayton, Ohio and Syracuse, New York
- two large cities—Detroit, Michigan and Los Angeles, California
- one super-city—New York City.

Each case study contains a brief background of the city and the department, as well as a description of that particular team program.

The case studies are not in-depth evaluations. They are reportorial accounts of the team policing experience in seven cities, with some subjective assessments made by persons on the scene. Efforts at more scientific evaluation were made in several of the cities, but since the team policing projects described were not planned and carried out under controlled experimental conditions, the opportunities for meaningful evaluation were limited. Recently in a number of cities, most notably Cincinnati, carefully planned and controlled team policing experiments have begun. By measuring pre-existing conditions and by collecting pertinent data during a period of controlled operations, these projects have the potential of producing reliable and useful evaluation results. Those experiments had not begun, however, when the authors were doing the field work for these case studies.

One of the goals of the Police Foundation is to provide better information about improvement programs developed in police departments around the country. Most police publications tell of new ideas and programs, but in a manner flattering to the creator of the programs. Discussion of the problems involved in implementing the innovation is usually avoided. Police administrators need to know the bad points as well as the good points of these programs in order to consider adopting them.

Team policing has clearly suffered from this problem of poor information exchange. Originally heralded with a great deal of favorable publicity, it has since become the subject of controversy in several parts of the country. The federal government's Law Enforcement Assistance Administration's 1970-71 Discretionary Grant Program specifically made funds available for team policing projects, and Model Cities funds have also been used to support such efforts in model city neighborhoods. Despite the favorable publicity, however, many police administrators have viewed team policing as a fad which has some merits in theory but is impossible to implement. Given the flow of both negative and positive reports, municipal government and police officials might understandably be confused as to just what team policing is all about. With objective and detailed information, however, more serious consideration of the idea could take place.

This book is intended to provide that information as a general introduction to team policing. We hope that police chiefs and planning directors, mayors, city managers, social scientists and others will use this as an aid to deciding whether team policing might be appropriate for their own communities. For those who do decide to implement neighborhood team policing, we recommend the prescriptive package published by the Law Enforcement Assistance Administration, *Neighborhood Team Policing* by Peter B. Bloch and David I. Specht. Their book is a practitioner's guide to the problems and processes of team policing. (It is available from the National Criminal Justice Reference Service, Washington, D.C. 20530.)

The first chapter of this book is an analysis of the elements of team policing. Chapter II presents descriptive case studies of team policing programs in seven different cities. The planning of team policing, the attempts to implement it, and the obstacles to its proper implementation are discussed in subsequent chapters. Chapter VI, on evaluations, suggests that well planned and controlled evaluations are difficult to achieve but that, whatever the quality of the evaluations and whatever the difficulties in changing police organizations, team policing programs have had many benefits.

The data for this study was gathered over a two-year period. From February to June 1971, Lawrence Sherman (while serving as an Alfred P. Sloane Foundation New York City Urban Fellow) performed an informal monitoring of the Neighborhood Police Team program in New York City for Police Commissioner Patrick V. Murphy. During the summer of 1971, the Police Foundation sent Mr. Sherman to Detroit, Michigan; Dayton, Ohio; Holyoke, Massachusetts; Syracuse, New York and Los Angeles, California, to review team programs. Each city was studied for two to six days, with at least 16 hours on patrol in each. Police officials at all levels were interviewed, as well as community leaders and residents, and relevant documents were reviewed.

Follow-up data was collected for the study in the fall of 1972 by Thomas Kelly, a free-lance journalist. In addition to the cities previously visited, Mr. Kelly also went to Richmond, California and studied the new Venice program in Los Angeles. Catherine Milton, Assistant Director of the Police Foundation, provided additional data on New York, Los Angeles, and Richmond.

Robert Wasserman, an administrative assistant to Chief Igleburger before the team program there was implemented and presently Director of Training and Education for the Boston Police Department, contributed additional data on the Dayton project and wrote that case study. Thomas McBride, former Police Foundation Staff Director, provided assistance throughout the research and writing and particularly contributed to the chapter on evaluations. Susan Michaelson, a consultant to the Police Foundation, provided research and editorial assistance throughout. The analysis and conceptualizations are primarily the contribution of Lawrence Sherman.

Chapter I
Elements of
Team Policing

Police administrators in the 1960's confronted a dilemma in organizing their departments: the community wanted both more sensitive police and better crime control. Police administrators who attempted to professionalize their departments through more centralized control and motorized patrol were criticized by community leaders and riot commissions for having police who were insensitive to and isolated from the communities they were supposed to serve. Yet with rising crime rates, few police administrators could seriously consider a return to the inefficiencies of the traditional beat-cop. Team policing was one answer to this conflict of police goals and needs.

By the early 1970's team policing had become a popular idea among many police administrators. And yet, even now, no one really knows what it is, what it costs, or whether it is an improvement. This study cannot answer those questions; it can only describe what it looks like in a few cities.

Team policing is a term that has meant something different in every city in which it has been tried. But all of the team policing programs studied for this book—except Richmond—attempted to implement three basic operational elements which differ from conventional patrol concepts. These three elements are: geographic stability of patrol, maximum interaction among team members, and maximum communication among team members and the community.

1. *Geographic stability of patrol: i.e., permanent assignment of teams of police to small neighborhoods.* The geographic stability of patrol is the most basic element. The only city which did not assign its teams permanently to a neighborhood was Richmond, California. There, teams were assigned as units on staggered shifts. Each team remained on duty for eight hours, and a new team came on duty every four hours. We included Richmond in this study, however, because that city is small enough to function as a neighborhood and because the patrol officers function as team members in much the same way as those geographically-based teams, despite the assignment by time.

2. *Maximum interaction among team members, including close internal communication among all officers assigned to an area during a 24-hour period, seven days a week.* The element of encouraging interaction among team members was evident in all the team policing cities, but with considerable variation. Implicit in the concept of maximum interaction is exchange of information. One of the simplest means of accomplishing this exchange is through the scheduling of team conferences at regular intervals. Analogies may be found in the case conferences conducted by social workers or doctors, in which each professional describes several difficult cases of the previous week and opens them to discussion with his colleagues, soliciting criticism and advice. The police teams which followed a similar route with their conferences found that, in many instances, the cases were continuing problems covering more than one shift and required cooperation among several police officers. Those teams which did not have formal conferences had to rely on informal ways of communicating—a practice which was more successful when the team was stationed and thereby isolated in a separate building than when sharing a stationhouse with the regular patrol units. The other critical factor in communication was the team leader. When he encouraged sharing of information and was able to instill a sense of teamsmanship, the members communicated more frequently and informally.

3. *Maximum communication among team members and the community.* The third element, maximum communication among team members and members of the community, seemed to be aided by regular meetings between teams and the community. These meetings were a means of emphasizing the cooperative aspects of the peacekeeping function, facilitating the flow of information, and assisting in the identification of community problems. Such conferences have been a

vehicle for eliciting community involvement in the police function. Another technique, participation of community members in police work, has been accomplished through auxiliary patrols, supply of information leading to arrests, and community voice in police policy-making. Such participation was designed to bring the police and community together in a spirit of cooperation. Finally, maximum communication among teams and the community has also been enhanced by an efficient system of referral of non-police problems (e.g., emotional problems, garbage collection, drug addiction) to appropriate service agencies. Teams that have developed their own neighborhood lists of social service units and names of social workers have made appropriate referrals far more quickly than through centralized traditional channels.

All of the cities in this study (except Richmond) attempted to achieve all three basic operational elements. The departments which were most successful in implementing these elements also had in common certain organizational supports: unity of supervision, lower-level flexibility in policy-making, unified delivery of services, and combined investigative and patrol functions.

1. *Unity of supervision.* Different supervisors controlling an area during the course of a day can create inconsistent police policies and approaches to community problems. It may be difficult, for example, for a group of young boys to understand why one police officer allows them to play baseball in the street between 8:00 a.m. and 4:00 p.m. while another forbids ball-playing from 4:00 p.m. to midnight. In order to maintain coherent and consistent police performance, then, it is preferable that one supervisor be responsible for a given area at all times and that his orders be obeyed. Unity of supervision is also useful for the effective performance of the officers as a team. If a team member has more than one supervisor giving him conflicting orders, he may determine that team policy-making is a myth and that the whole team concept is a hoax.

2. *Lower-level flexibility in policy-making.* Interaction among team members is most productive when the team has the flexibility to carry out its own operational decisions. Indeed, the very rationale for the sharing of information among team members is that they will use their increased knowledge to decide upon better strategies for the delivery of police services to their neighborhood. For example, decisions about mode of dress and duty schedules have been traditionally

reserved for higher-ups, but several departments pushed those decisions down to the team level where information about neighborhood needs was most accurate.

The police administrators who advocated increased authority at lower levels of the hierarchy considered it a means of increasing responsibility and accountability of patrol officers. Former New York City Police Commissioner Patrick Murphy, for example, tried to loosen the strict rules governing behavior at all ranks in order to discourage "buck-passing" up the ranks. Supervisors at the precinct level were held accountable for the performance of patrol officers in their precincts, team leaders for their team members, team officers for themselves.

3. *Unified delivery of services.* Some departments extended the concept of team decision-making to complete control over the delivery of all police services in the team neighborhood. This included the team's power to decide when specialized police units were needed or when they would be disruptive. This concept was also designed to make the best use of local community knowledge developed by the officers who patrol an area every day. It does not deny the value of specialist skills, but stresses the ability of the local police generalist to decide when they are needed.

4. *Combined investigative and patrol functions.* In the absence of information supplied by the community, apprehension of a criminal is difficult. As a part of the larger unified delivery of services, team programs should seek to combine patrol and investigative functions, for the intuitive judgments required for effective investigations are enhanced by familiarity with the life of the community. As Egon Bittner has observed:

> To give circumstantial factors their correct weight in decision making it is necessary that they be intelligently appraised. That is, patrolmen must be able to draw on background information to be able to discern what particular constellations of facts and factors mean. In the case of the carefully deliberate policeman—by which is meant a man who organizes his activities with a view towards long-range peacekeeping and crime control objectives in the area of his patrol, knowing that what he does from case to case can create more or less calculable advantages or liabilities for himself in the future—the background information consists of an enormously detailed factual knowledge.[1]

---

[1] Egon Bittner, *The Functions of the Police in Modern Society* (National Institute of Mental Health, November 1970), p. 90.

When one considers that crimes of violence are usually committed by people known to the victim, it becomes clear that a knowledge of the human relationships in a community is of immeasurable value in solving crimes. It is instructive, though, that Bittner had to note the "case of the carefully deliberate policeman" as an exception to the rule. The cultivation of area knowledge has not been something for which the patrol officer has been rewarded in the United States. By contrast, an essential element in the English Unit Beat scheme is the "collator," the central receiver of daily area reports; each officer is evaluated partly according to how much quality information he feeds the collator.

The seven case studies that follow will describe the team policing programs in each city and the contexts in which they developed. Each will also discuss the three basic operational elements and four organizational supports of team policing in each city.

SUMMARY OF ELEMENTS
(The following summarizes the elements of team policing in each city.)

Operational Elements	Dayton	Detroit	New York	Syracuse	Holyoke	Los Angeles (Venice)	Richmond
Stable geographic assignment	+	+	-	+	+	+	•
Intra-team interaction	-	+	-	-	+	+	+
Formal team conferences	-	+	-	-	+	+	+
Police-community communication	+	+	-	-	+	+	•
Formal community conferences	+	•	•	-	+	+	•
Community participation in police work	+	+	+	•	+	+	•
Systematic referrals to social agencies	+	-	-	•	•	•	+
Organizational Supports							
Unity of supervision	+	+	-	+	+	+	+
Lower-level flexibility	-	-	-	+	+	+	+
Unified delivery of services	+	-	-	+	+	+	•
Combined patrol and investigative functions	+	+	•	+	+	+	+

Key:
+ the element was planned and realized
- the element was planned but not realized
• the element was not planned

7

Chapter II
Case Studies

Dayton

The development of team policing in Dayton, Ohio was the result of numerous factors, most notably the commitment of the police chief to massive police improvement and alteration of the police role. The tense racial situation in the city, coupled with the necessity for the police department to make significant improvements in its delivery of service with no additional manpower, were important reasons for the development of one of the country's first team policing experiments.

The City

The City of Dayton, in southern Ohio, with a population of about 250,000, is the center of a metropolitan area of 850,000. An industrial city, it is the headquarters of the National Cash Register Company, and has such large industries as Chrysler Airtemp Division and the Frigidaire Division of General Motors. It is a labor town with a large working-class population dependent upon these industries' success for their own livelihood. While Dayton has had one of the highest industrial wage bases in the Ohio region, there have been frequent periods of economic decline and fairly substantial labor strife.

In many ways, the city is a North/South border city. Over 35% of the city's population is black, and the percentage is steadily increasing. A large percentage of the white population is of Appalachian background, having moved north from Kentucky and Tennessee and settled in Dayton where employment opportunities seemed good.

Like so many cities throughout the country, Dayton was shaken by the social unrest of the 1960's. These tensions broke out into civil disorder for three successive years, necessitating several responses by the Ohio National Guard. The causes of this urban unrest were viewed as racial militance by a large segment of the community, with little discussion by the community of underlying factors, such as poor schools, unemployment, and general urban decay.

The Police Department

During the Sixties, the Dayton Police Department was a fairly modern, technically proficient operation. Having moved into a new Safety Building in 1955, the mechanical systems of the department were considered modern and generally sufficient for the accomplishment of the police mission as it was then perceived. Through the years, the department had moved with the times, reorganizing itself as the need arose and generally keeping itself in line with current police thinking. While never an innovator in the police field, the department was quick to adopt new techniques of policing, such as establishment of a police-community relations unit, modernization of the radio communications system, establishment of a crime laboratory, and provision of a modern line-staff organizational structure. Indeed, most Dayton police officers considered themselves members of an outstanding department that could match most others found throughout the country. Generally the white community agreed and the black community was silent.

But with the disorders of the 1960's, the image of the department was somewhat tarnished. While the department prided itself on the fact that each disorder had been controlled without a loss of life, two of them had been precipitated by violence involving the police, and the minority community believed that police brutality was a serious problem.

Additionally, there was little black representation on the police force. By 1968, there was only one black sergeant (who retired shortly thereafter) and approximately 25 black officers—less than 6% of the total force. This became a community issue within the minority community, since over 30% of the community was then black. Significantly, a large number of police officers had Appalachian backgrounds and were perceived as being insensitive to community problems in black areas.

It was during this period of turmoil that a new city manager, Graham Watt, arrived in Dayton, faced with the task of selecting a new chief of police to replace the recently retired one. After intensive interviewing and testing of candidates, he selected Robert M. Igleburger as the new chief. Igleburger, then 57 years old and serving as Superintendent of Operations, was the senior ranking police officer under the acting chief.

It was the appointment of Igleburger that led to a series of major changes in the Dayton Police Department and the institution of various new programs, among which was the team policing project. Team policing, as well as the many other programs that were undertaken during his tenure, was aimed at moving the police department toward Igleburger's conception of policing, responsive to the newly

12

surfacing problems of the Dayton community.

Shortly after the appointment, Igleburger was faced with several community crises which impressed upon him the degree of community anger over certain aspects of police performance. The steps Igleburger took were considered swift and drastic. He hired a young graduate student from Michigan State University as his civilian administrative assistant. With his new aide providing the needed staff work, he reorganized the police department to reallocate resources to handle recent large increases in crime, installed a new computer to analyze data from police officers' reports, increased patrol visibility, reduced detective bureaucratic red-tape, and instituted many other operational reforms.

Yet, the most important part of the chief's efforts concerned improvement of the community relationship. Igleburger saw the police role drastically changing; he felt that community conditions necessitated changes in the police role and the manner in which police service was delivered.

Throughout this initial period, the chief became increasingly committed to the concept of neighborhood integrity, a concept that became the basis of his team policing efforts. When a group of Dayton residents demanded the formation of a city-wide police auxiliary, the chief refused; as an alternative, he offered to assist them in creating neighborhood-oriented auxiliaries. His distaste for city-wide auxiliaries was based on a belief that the city could ill afford to have auxiliaries, of necessity less well-trained than regular police officers, patrolling areas in which racial tension between police and community was at a high level and which had cultures they did not understand.

Also, the chief established a policy of permitting citizens to ride in police cars during all tours of duty, providing the citizen rode only in the area in which he lived. In this manner, Igleburger moved to develop a strategy of neighborhood integrity and a commitment toward citizen involvement in their own neighborhoods.

The commitment to the community was carried into the new recruit training program for new police officers. Each new recruit officer was required to spend the initial four weeks of his training in various community agencies throughout the city learning about community life among cultural groups different from his own. Through these experiences—in a black high school, a welfare office, an Appalachian community center, a state hospital, and a black social service agency, for example—the recruits began to better understand the importance of community identification and the necessity for the police to adapt to differing lifestyles throughout the city.

The development of team policing grew out of this commitment to neighborhood integrity and community involvement. Once these concepts were firmly established, large amounts of federal funding became available for program development and implementation. Two primary program efforts were undertaken. The first—a conflict management orientation to policing—provided the theoretical framework for the development of the second, team policing.

The Experimental Neighborhood

During this period, the basic conflicts in Dayton revolved around race; the primary tensions were between blacks and Appalachians. These problems were well reflected in a neighborhood called Daytonview. Heavily black on its south side, bordering the totally black west side of Dayton, the neighborhood turned increasingly white to the north, until in the northernmost section it was an upper-class white neighborhood.

The neighborhood had been the object of a federally-funded "stabilization program." As more blacks had moved in, whites had increasingly fled to suburban communities, a movement the stabilization program aimed at reducing. There were significant hostilities between blacks and whites in many parts of the neighborhood, especially in the areas undergoing a transition from predominantly white to predominantly black. These hostilities extended to blacks and whites in the neighborhood schools.

The Design of the Team Policing Program

In late summer of 1969, one of Igleburger's aides, while attending a conference at the University of Wisconsin Law School, mentioned to an official of the National Institute of Law Enforcement and Criminal Justice of LEAA that Dayton had some ideas on model programs. One of the ideas was for a group of police officers, operating in a definable neighborhood, to have total responsibility for policing activities, with the assistance of para-professional neighborhood workers. The Institute dispatched a staff member to Dayton to assess program potential, and it agreed to accept a proposal from Dayton for a model program as part of an initial Pilot Cities project.

14

The idea presented to the Institute was not new, however. Based upon a visit by Igleburger's administrative assistant to Syracuse to view the new Crime Control Teams operating there, the department had concluded that the team approach—that is, the formation of patrol officers into teams with beat accountability—was an exciting and valid method of improving police service. But the department was dissatisfied with the crime control emphasis of Syracuse; Igleburger believed that a broader policing orientation was needed.

The resulting plan for team policing had three primary goals:

1. To test the effectiveness of the generalist-specialist approach to police service delivery;

2. To produce a community-oriented police structure that would be responsive to differing neighborhood lifestyles; and

3. To alter the bureaucratic police structure away from the militaristic model toward a neighborhood-oriented professional model.

These goals reflected the commitment of the chief to a new policing orientation; implementation of the program toward achieving these goals had a number of parts.

First, a team of about forty volunteer patrolmen, four sergeants, and a team leader would be assigned total responsibility for all police activities in the experimental district, later referred to as the Fifth District (basically the Daytonview neighborhood). These officers would operate as generalist-specialists; that is, each officer would have a level of operational competence sufficient to deal with all the routine problems that came to his attention. Additionally, each member of the team would have a specialty in which he would receive additional training. In this manner, while each officer would be a competent generalist, he would also have a needed specialty. Within a given team, a wide range of specialties—such as youth problem resolution, family crisis intervention, and complex investigative strategy—would be available among team members.

Specialists from the department would not operate in the District, unless in response to a request from a team member. When a member of a team encountered a problem requiring skill beyond that which he normally possessed as a generalist, he would call on the services of the team member having that skill.

The entire program was to be community-oriented. The training

15

and orientation program was designed to provide each team member with a thorough understanding of the cultural backgrounds and life-styles of major groups in the Daytonview neighborhood. This training and orientation plan included a live-in experience for each team member with a neighborhood family. It was assumed that through these experiences, officers would develop community contacts and better understand community priorities and problems.

Preventive patrol was to be eliminated to enable members of the team to undertake problem-oriented activities. By eliminating this requirement for patrol, time was to be available for officer-initiated activities that would permit exercise of individual officer discretion in dealing with the community, establishing relationships with opinion-makers, and constructively dealing with issues of concern to neighborhood residents. Although preventive patrol was to be eliminated, officers would be spending sufficient time in those areas having problems for their presence still to be felt.

Additionally, it was planned that the teams would have a great deal of discretion in determining things such as uniforms, vehicle utilization, and scheduling. The program called for team decision-making as the basis for being able to hold the members accountable for their later actions.

The proposal also called for the employment of para-professional civilian employees to assist team members in the delivery of non-criminal service. The already existing Neighborhood Assistance Officers (the neighborhood-oriented police auxiliary) would also participate in various service delivery and crime detection and prevention activities. Through the utilization of para-professionals and auxiliary officers who lived in the neighborhood, it was expected that a significant amount of the responsibility for police service delivery could be transferred to the community, thus increasing their understanding of police problems and providing a broader base of community support for police activities.

Finally, it was planned that working hours would be flexible to better permit officers to undertake creative activities to deal with community problems and needs. It was also planned that the Neighborhood Assistance Council overseeing the then-existing neighborhood auxiliary would be expanded (especially to include more black and poor members) and would serve as a policy advisory committee for the new policing operation. Furthermore, it was agreed that this committee would have significant input to the determination of which police commander became the team leader.

Program Implementation

Thirty-nine team members were finally selected from about 80 volunteers. The community, through both traditional spokesmen and the Neighborhood Assistance Council was asked to review the list of prospective team members and object to any they wished. Although they objected to two, the chief dropped only one. Similarly, the Neighborhood Council was given the option of reviewing volunteers for the position of team leader. There were only two volunteers; both were generally acceptable and the one who lived in the neighborhood was selected.

The original plan was to introduce the team by having its individual members live with neighborhood families for a short time. The families were to be paid, but arrangements were difficult—few black families could be found who were willing to accept any of the team members as guests, so the idea was dropped.

The team began with only two black officers. It would have been difficult to have had a more fully integrated team, since there were only 28 black officers in the entire department. In time, these two black officers were transferred from the team at their own request as racial tensions mounted within the department.

The team members were provided with an intensive training program, concentrating on conflict management skills, the role of the team in the neighborhood, and utilization of various neighborhood resources to improve service delivery. The training itself was an experimental undertaking by a New York psychological firm. It concentrated upon conversion of the participating officers into generalist-specialists. However, no time was spent developing the team into a working unit.

Two years after it had begun operating, the team had some 60 men divided into four platoons, with a lieutenant as team commander. Each platoon had its own sergeant and coordinator, and each in theory had its own special section of the District. In fact, cars on patrol answered calls for the whole area, and the officers in the car decided where they would spend most of their uneventful hours. The platoons were well below their paper strength—as a result of both fiscal austerity and internal departmental conflict over promotions and recruiting. A platoon which was to have 15 officers had only 10 or 12. Neither the department nor the Fifth District had achieved any remarkable shift away from the military-style operation toward the decentralized and democratic model. The hoped-for withering away of rank and uniforms did not develop. The chief urged new approaches, including variety in dress, to the team's first commander, but generally traditional patterns of operation were utilized.

The first team commander retired and was succeeded by a lieutenant somewhat more disposed to innovation. The team members could wear blazers and slacks, but they seldom did. Civilian clothes were worn only during follow-up investigations; the officers preferred uniforms, especially at night, because of their high visibility.

The Fifth District was directly linked to headquarters, with the lieutenant reporting directly to the chief, a process which tended to depart from the military hierarchy. But because the central dispatcher still controlled the assignments of the Fifth District's patrol cars, the frequent dispatching of team cars out of the neighborhoods on other calls made it difficult to build neighborhood links or maintain neighborhood integrity. Finally, the introduction of a system of "priorities"—which would hold out-of-District calls of lesser urgency for out-of-District cars—improved the situation. The hope that the entire team would meet frequently to discuss common problems and engage in a sort of participatory management was not realized. While the original intent was to give off-duty officers overtime pay to attend these meetings, the fiscal difficulties of the city made this impractical and attendance fell off sharply. The team commander said later that the meetings had become mere "bitching sessions" and had contributed to dissension rather than to the pursuit of common goals.

The team was headquartered in the basement of an old apartment building. The team quarters were more than adequate, with a very large community room, kitchen facilities and rows of movable chairs. There were nine other rooms, ranging from cubicles to the team commander's large office. While it was less formal and forbidding than the standard police precinct, it was less informal and inviting than a storefront type of headquarters.

Civilians and the Team

The members of the Dayton team did have a strong rapport with one segment of the community—the civilian volunteers known as

Neighborhood Assistance Officers (NAO's). NAO's did a great many of the routine tasks which police have historically, if reluctantly, assumed. They were men and women from the neighborhood who volunteered to spend several scheduled hours a week patrolling the neighborhoods in their own automobiles. They wore uniforms distinguished from the regular patrol officers', and they had written instructions to stay away from situations with a potential for violence and from the investigation of crimes. One man in the District was paid a modest sum for working as the NAO coordinator. The NAO scheme existed independently of the team plan, and there were NAO's in districts which did not have teams. There were 37 NAO's in the Fifth District, including a shop foreman, engineer, florist, dietician, nurse, para-medic technician, insurance man, and several factory workers. Eight of the NAO's were black. There were also eight women, six of whom were married. Although the majority of NAO's were middle-aged householders, six were under thirty and one was over fifty.

It was suggested by some critics of neighborhood auxiliaries that since the volunteers were not paid and were, consequently, under less realistic discipline than police officers, they might follow their "natural inclinations," inconsistent with departmental policies or the law. The department provided fairly good guidance and control, however, and the use of NAO's to some degree enabled the police to shift their energies to primary police work rather than ancillary activities.

Some secondary goals were implicit in the Dayton experiment. In theory the new team police were to have been in touch frequently and substantially with public and private social service organizations. The bulletin board in the community room at the team headquarters had the picture of nine young YMCA community workers permanently posted. Five were black, four were white, and few were apparently ever called by the officers. On the other hand, the police department had a contract with the Good Samaritan Mental Health Center, and the team members diverted a good many domestic conflict cases to Good Samaritan counselors. The practice was for the police to handle initial domestic calls themselves but to refer repeaters to the counselors. In early 1973, the counselors were averaging 26 such calls a month in District Five.

Program Assessment

Clearly, the Dayton team policing program ended up being somewhat different from what was originally proposed. A number of the proposed program elements were never accomplished. There were no community live-in situations. Patrol officers were not really involved in the selection of their supervisors, although they could veto their sergeants and successfully had one removed. The militaristic structure of the organization was not eliminated. And the generalist-specialist model was never adequately tested.

There are a number of reasons why the program encountered difficulties. Important was the fact that the program espoused policing principles quite different from the O.W. Wilson type of teachings that dominated police thinking during that period. Additionally, a high level of community tension and turmoil existed during the implementation period. A great deal of attention was being focused on the police department as it was being called upon to deal with various community crises. School disorders were widespread, racial conflict in integrated neighborhoods was commonplace, and citizen fear of minority group population movement was at a high level.

Coupled with this conflict was the fiscal crisis faced by the city. Having voted down a city income tax numerous times, the city was forced to adopt stringent austerity measures, including a no-hire policy and, in some cases, governmental worker lay-offs. This draining of public resources alone was sufficient to severely tax the ability of the police department to deliver services. The implementation of new programs only further drained available resources.

But probably most important was the lack of understanding within the department and in some segments of the community of Chief Igleburger's commitment to change. The directions for change initiated by the chief were threatening to many officers and citizens, especially among those who failed to comprehend the practical orientation of the proposed changes in the police role. The changes Igleburger sought to introduce into the policing style were perceived as left-wing liberal attempts to undermine law and order in the city, rather than sincere attempts to equip the department to better respond to community conflict during a period of social change.

The team policing concept itself was controversial, especially since it proposed to challenge the traditional military structure of policing, alter the common relationship between police and community, and provide greater discretion among lower-level police officers. But had the program been perceived as dealing with those issues alone, it would have had better success. But instead, it became entangled in the controversy surrounding the complex racial conflicts within and without the department.

Finally, the large number of programs that were being implemented at the same time created an atmosphere of instability within the department. While the change being brought about was valid, the means of implementation and the quality of planning could probably have been improved.

Clearly, however, the Dayton team policing program served a valuable function in testing a number of important concepts aimed at improvement of police service delivery within complex urban neighborhoods. Given better planning and a less complicated environment, this policing model would seem to be an effective way of improving a policy agency's relationship with and responsiveness to center city neighborhoods.

Leaning on the lessons of the team policing experiment, Igleburger (now retired) moved ahead in institutionalizing some of the original program concepts. For example, he decentralized his patrol force, assigning four of his five captains to neighborhood policing command responsibilities. Additionally, he aggressively moved forward with the demilitarization of the organization, eliminating ranks, combining positions, and increasing the commitment of the lower-level personnel in the decision-making process. (The department is presently being sued by two sergeants to stop the demilitarization process, but former Chief Igleburger does not expect the suit to succeed.) Finally, he began a community-oriented policy-making process that brings together groups of police officers and citizens to jointly develop police policy statements on matters of mutual concern.

The Elements

In terms of the elements analyzed in Chapter I, the Dayton experience was this:

1. The basic element of team policing, geographic stability of assignment, was violated in two ways: initially, the team cars were frequently dispatched beyond the boundaries of the Fifth District (although this problem was later alleviated), and they ignored the team boundaries within the District. District boundaries were ultimately respected, however.

2. Interaction among the team members took place primarily in

writing, along with some informal association. Few formal team conferences were held.

3. Communication with the community was more issue-oriented under the team policing program than it had been before, mostly through monthly meetings. Street contacts were different, primarily because of a personnel shortage rather than the team policing program itself. Officers throughout the city made more use of informal disposition of many matters, if only to save time. Referral systems to social agencies were established, and some use was made of the referral systems by the team members. The strongest community participation factor was the NAO program.

As for the four organizational supports:

1. Team leadership was weak but unity of supervision was maintained.

2. Formal and theoretical flexibility of policy-making was allowed the teams in terms of scheduling, uniforms and tactics, but was never fully employed. The teams were content with traditional practices.

3. All police problems in the District were handled by the teams, so that unified delivery of services was achieved.

4. The team members performed both patrol and investigative functions.

Thus, while failing to meet its ambitious goals of demilitarization, the program did achieve a generalist model and a more community-oriented structure.

Detroit

Detroit is a city of 1.5 million people, the fifth largest in the country. In 1971 almost half of its residents were black and the rest were largely blue collar, white foreign stock and white Southerners. Almost half of the inner-city households had incomes of less than $3,000, and 50% of the ghetto's adolescents were out of school and out of work.

The crime rate in Detroit matched the population—the fifth highest in the nation. The homicide rate was high and a rapidly growing narcotics trade had created a series of murderous gang wars between competing drug distributors. The city still had a hangover of fear and distrust from the 1967 riots, in which 43 people died and $50 million worth of property was destroyed. Though one effect of the riot's aftermath was increased economic opportunities for blacks, another was a large emigration of white families to the suburbs. Many of those who stayed bought guns.

The Department

When the Beat Commander (team) program began in 1970, the Detroit Police Department had an authorized strength of 5,659 uniformed officers, 527 civilians and 150 cadets. The actual strength was 4,583 uniformed, 448 civilians, and 119 cadets, a total of 5,150. The patrol officer's salary was $12,000 after four years' service. The average age in the department was 35 and the average educational level was not very high; only one-fourth of the officers had ever taken college courses. About 12% of the force was black (in 1965 it had been only 3%).

The department's personality has been described as "fraternal." Detroit mayors have historically appointed non-policemen to the job of police commissioner, and this has had the effect of unifying the uniformed force against outside civilians appointed by City Hall. The Detroit Police Officers Association has been so strong that it has often received credit (and blame) for running the department. In early 1967 it organized a "blue flu" police strike that kept 1,000 officers home and won a substantial wage increase (from $8,335 to $10,000). Through skillful collective bargaining it had gained much control in the 1960's over police organization and methods. The fraternal aspect of the department was not absolute, however; there was a good deal of racial conflict within. As one high official put it, "The blacks and whites in the police department do not know each other—they seem to speak a different language."

The Team

When Roman Gribbs became Detroit's Mayor in 1970, he appointed Patrick V. Murphy, formerly LEAA Administrator and Washington, D.C. Public Safety Director, as his Police Commissioner. One of Murphy's first acts was to initiate the Beat Commander Project, an experiment in team policing. The Beat Commander Project was designed to reduce crime, to increase public willingness to report crimes and to serve as witnesses, to involve the patrol officers in a particular neighborhood, to give greater responsibility to sergeants, and to increase accountability for police performance. In March of 1970 Sergeant Ferdinand Kuchinsky was assigned as the beat commander of a team of 20 scout car and foot patrol officers. As beat commander, he was responsible around the clock for two radio car territories of Detroit's busy 10th Precinct, a middle- and lower-class black residential area containing some 15,000 people in one square mile. Kuchinsky was given unusual authority. He could schedule tours of duty in accordance with workload, assign officers at will, and bring them together for monthly conferences. Three detectives from the precinct squad were assigned to work closely with the Beat Command area. Soon it was obvious that the beat commander would have to work a minimum of 60 to 70 hours a week to provide adquate supervision, so in June of 1970 Sergeant Leroy Charrier became assistant beat commander. While regular watch sergeants still supervised the Beat Command area when neither Kuchinsky nor Charrier was on duty, the assignment of the second sergeant improved the unity of supervision for field operations. In early 1971 a third sergeant was assigned to the Beat Command in order to test the value of a higher proportion of sergeants to patrol officers. Together, the three supervisors were expected to provide almost complete 24-hour supervision in the Beat Command. Sergeant Kuchinsky still held primary authority.

Team operations continued fairly successfully into late 1971. Then, after three precinct commanders had progressively proscribed the team's flexibility, the team died a slow death (as an operationally distinct unit) and eventually merged back into the standard precinct

24

patrols. In spite of the general hostility of 10th Precinct patrol officers and most of the middle management to the program, however, it did not die in disgrace. A carefully conducted evaluation suggested that even if it did not reduce crime, it was a superior form of organization on a number of other measures.

Commissioner Murphy had developed the idea for a Beat Commander Project in 1969 when he was Director of Public Safety Research at the Urban Institute. After his appointment as Police Commissioner in Detroit and the decision to implement the Beat Commander Project, arrangements were made with the Urban Institute to provide assistance in evaluating the project. Peter Bloch of the Urban Institute staff served as director of this evaluation and also was involved in planning the project, writing operational guidelines for the team, and orienting the team members to the Beat Commander concept. Efforts to keep the project pure in an experimental sense encountered much resistance, both from radio dispatchers who dispatched team cars out of the experimental area and precinct officials and others in the department who interfered with the autonomy of the beat commander. The evaluation concluded that the Beat Commander Project was successful in some of its objectives—team cars responded more rapidly to calls than did non-team cars, better communication was established with the people in the team neighborhood, the morale of team members was high, and the team cars answered more radio calls and made better quality arrests than did other elements of the patrol force.[2]

Commissioner Murphy, however, left to become Police Commissioner in New York City in October 1970, and his successor and the command staff of the Detroit Police Department apparently felt that the Beat Commander Project had drawbacks, particularly in manpower allocation, sufficient to render it undesirable as a general design for the patrol force.

The present Commissioner, John F. Nichols, explains the inability of the department to support the operation largely as a result of manpower costs, but also as a result of the following contributing factors:[3]

---

[2]Peter B. Bloch and Cyrus Ulberg, "The Beat Commander Concept," *The Police Chief*, September 1972. The Urban Institute evaluation conclusions were based upon a survey of all officers associated with the project, police records, interviews, observations by Urban Institute staff, and reactions (not a survey) of citizens in the Beat Command neighborhood.

[3]Letter to Mr. Thomas F. McBride, former Staff Director of the Police Foundation, May 16, 1973.

First, the department was not sufficiently educated or advised of the intent, purpose, mission, and concept of the Beat Commander Project.

Second, the personnel selected were hand-picked, and whether we like to recognize this fact or not, very often this, and this alone, controls its acceptability among peers. We all know the Hawthorne effect.

Thirdly, no controls were set or were built into the evaluation process, so it was difficult to ascertain, other than by adjectival, subjective evaluation, the effectiveness or lack of effectiveness except in statistical analysis such as sick days and response time which may very well have been experienced because of the hand selection of the officers. The evaluation being performed by an individual long associated with the project and with vested interests would no doubt be questioned by some.

There is no doubt in my mind that the concept is a fine and supportable one. There was, and still is, however, doubt in my mind as to whether or not the isolation of segments of a precinct or the delivery of a different type of police service to one segment of the precinct or one segment of the city, for that matter, is a supportable proposition in terms of a city-wide responsibility. (The manpower commitments precluded implementation over a broader base.)

One of the major benefits we found was in the supervisor-patrolman relationship that resulted. To this end, we adjusted our span of control and assigned personal responsibilities to sergeants for specific men so that they became familiar both with their area and with the manpower in that area.

The Elements

To summarize: although it was accomplished only after a great struggle, the Beat Command Project did achieve the first operational element—stability of assignment.

Interaction among team members was achieved with less difficulty. Conferences were held frequently, at first weekly and later on a monthly basis, while informal communication continued during day-to-day operations.

Communication with the community was vigorously pursued, though not always with success. While Murphy and Bloch had hoped that the Beat Command team would make use of the resources provided by local community service agencies, effective liaison for referral systems was never established. Neither were public meetings held under the auspices of the Beat Command, although team members frequently attended community meetings and sometimes attended even meetings outside the Beat Command area. The team did make good use of the precinct's auxiliary program until middle management stopped it.

As for organizational supports: unity of supervision was guaranteed through the designation of one supervisor as first among three equals, and no outside sergeants supervised the team.

The flexibility of the team to set its own policy was theoretically large but in practice was hampered by the interference of middle management.

The Beat Commander was given complete authority for unified delivery of services and for all police problems on his beat, even to the extent of being able to request or forbid the presence of tactical units in his area. After strenuous objections by middle management, however, this control was reduced substantially.

Investigative functions were not combined with the duties of patrol, but they were accommodated to team organization through the assignment of three detectives to work solely with the Beat Command team.

New York

New York is the largest and most diverse city in the United States. Among its 8 million residents, about 60% are whites from every country in Europe—mostly Jews, Italians, and Irish—and the rest are from Puerto Rico, the American South, Haiti, Africa, China, India and almost every country in the world. While some neighborhoods have more of one ethnic group than another, there are no fixed boundaries between the groups. Few homogeneous "neighborhoods" in the traditional sense can be found, for the many ethnic groups are well distributed throughout the five boroughs.

The ethnic diversity is matched by geographical diversity. Manhattan is a mixture of office towers, penthouses, brownstones, and overcrowded tenements. The Bronx is an apartment-house suburb with some slums worse than Manhattan's. Brooklyn has miles of neat two-family houses with pockets of industry, urban renewal wastelands, and decaying slums. Queens and Staten Island are like many other single-family house suburbs, and they house many of the city's police. Indeed, geographic and ethnic diversity were reflected by—and a reason for—the selection of the sites for the first team experiments.

But with this diversity, there are many problems. Heroin addiction pervades all five boroughs and all walks of life. Street crime has made many people fearful of walking the city streets, even in daylight. Basic city services—health, sanitation, fire and, of course, police—have often been overloaded by alcoholics and the mentally ill, tons and tons of garbage, false alarms and firetrap housing, disputing families and gang violence.

As an administrative means of delivering better city services, and as a political means of giving local communities more power, New York under the Lindsay administration moved to decentralize much of city government. Local district boundaries for the various agencies were redrawn to coincide, and "neighborhood managers" were established in some districts to coordinate all city services. And the police department, while also involved in this joint decentralization effort, undertook an even greater decentralization of its own.

The Department

Founded in 1844, the New York City Police Department is the

oldest and largest police department in North America. Its 30,000 police officers are divided into 10 ranks. With three levels of civilian commissioners above the hierarchy of sworn personnel, the rank structure pyramid is as high as the entire U.S. Army's (salaries—$12,500 to $41,000—are even higher). The army has also been the traditional model for running the department, but the fraternal atmosphere of—and outside political influences on—"the job" has made it a far cry from the military. Repeated corruption scandals over the years led to the creation of many headquarters units which "spied" on the field, resulting in an abdication of responsibility by field commanders.

The reform administration of Commissioner Patrick V. Murphy, which began in the fall of 1970, sought to change this overall administrative style through a program of decentralization. The major thrust was to give more authority to field commanders at every level, which demanded greater accountability of the commanders for the performance of their officers. Few new structures were established by this program, leaving the rank hierarchy (fixed by state law) unchanged. But many new policies were established to change the relationships and division of decision-making labor among the ranks.

The major structural element in the program of decentralization was at the bottom of the hierarchy: the Neighborhood Police Teams. One of the first steps in the decentralization program was the redefinition of the relationship between patrol officers and sergeants. As one high official put it: "that order gave the sergeant more power than an assistant chief!" But formal power and real power turned out to be very different things.

The Teams

When Commissioner Murphy took up his New York post, he directed the Planning Division to develop for New York a project based on Detroit's Beat Commander Project. The result, inaugurated in January 1971, was the Neighborhood Police Team (NPT), an effort with objectives similar to those of the Beat Commander Project. The first team was established in one part of the 77th Precinct of Bedford-Stuyvesant, a black poverty area in Brooklyn, under the command of Sergeant William Ambrose. Additional teams were soon established in Harlem and middle-class areas of Queens and the North Bronx, and later in all patrol divisions and boroughs. By August of 1971 there were almost 30 teams totalling approximately 1,000 men. Beginning then, some neighborhood police teams were implemented on a precinct-wide basis. In January of 1972, NPT's were combined with the "Model Precinct" concept, whereby entire precinct were divided into team areas and managed with a number of innovative programs. Nonetheless, the department continued for the next year to implement teams in parts of precincts as a means of appeasing community anger at the closing of old precinct houses or at a particularly notorious crime. By 1973, there were teams—or there soon would be—in most precincts.

While the major goal of the New York project was crime control through improved community relations, a significant latent objective was to increase productivity through improved leadership and motivation. This was in fact accomplished, for the average time required to complete a radio run was drastically cut by the teams—at least initially.

The Neighborhood Police Team was similar to the Beat Command in Detroit. The first NPT consisted of 18 men assigned to one radio motor patrol sector (population about 10,000) performing both foot and car patrol. On the door of their car, a painted banner announced their presence: *Neighborhood Police Team.* Later, teams with 30 to 35 men covered two patrol sectors. One sergeant was assigned as the Neighborhood Police Chief. He was responsible at all times for the area, but other watch sergeants provided supervision of the team in the absence of the team commander. Detectives were not directly assigned to the NPT program (until the spring of 1973, and then only on a very small scale), although NPT officers were encouraged to take investigative initiative. The NPT chief could assign his officers to plainclothes or other duty and had wide latitude in scheduling and other decisions.

By August of 1971, the entire 34th Precinct in northern Manhattan was converted to the NPT system. The precinct was divided into five teams of about 30 to 35 men each in hopes (which were not realized) of preventing team cars from being called out of their team areas. Another element of the 34th Precinct experiment was establishment of the watch commander system, under which lieutenants, entitled "Operations Officers," played a more active supervisory role in field operations and performed less desk supervision of the precinct house. With such innovations as special training projects and streamlined clerical procedures, the "model precincts" (24th, 77th, 110th, and 50th) followed the same basic plan as the 34th Precinct.

Concentrated NPT training under a federal grant began for the five precincts in August 1972, with the first of two four-day sessions at the police academy on team management, crisis control and community dynamics. Following these sessions the training division began a continuing in-precinct training process in the same five precincts. Two trainers—one officer, one civilian—were assigned to each and they were encouraged to tailor their training to the needs of the particular team members. There was some resistance from precinct commanders, but this lessened in time. One precinct commander opposed efforts to train the officers in such skills as conflict control, and he insisted that the trainers concentrate on drilling the men in paper filing routines, but he was shortly transferred. The reception of the sergeants and the team members to the training effort was much more positive. "We were overwhelmed by their acceptance of us," one trainer said, and in most of the five precincts, training—and the trainers—became part of the ongoing life of the precinct.

The acceptance of team policing by the rest of the department was not so easy, however. Lieutenants who had been taken off desk duty and put on the street as operations officers (watch commanders concerned with all officers on one 8-hour shift) naturally collided with the NPT sergeants concerned with 24-hour area teams. Both had equal powers over their officers, at least theoretically. This specific problem was resolved by bringing lieutenants into the team structure as field coordinators of specific teams (in the all-team precincts).

But mid-management (lieutenants and above) were still generally the source of much resistance. The way teams worked depended not only on their own initiatives, but also on the freedom allowed them by the local "bosses," regardless of what the NPT guidelines were. To deal with this problem, NPT concept training for borough, division and precinct commanders was begun in late 1972.

Two other problems plagued the NPT's: continual assignment of team cars out of the team area and resentment of the team by non-team officers in the precinct. The latter problem may be solved by the possible conversion of the entire Patrol Bureau to team policing, so that NPT will not be an elite. But the problem of keeping team cars in their areas is far from resolved (see Chapter V).

Investigations were another area of limited success. Detectives were not assigned to the NPT's even on an experimental basis until the spring of 1973. NPT patrol officers were always supposed to have done investigative work. Some teams did much of it, but most did not. The resistance of the politically powerful detective force makes any merger of patrol and investigative functions in the same officer a very difficult task indeed: in July of 1973 the detective union went to court to oppose a simple transfer of half their numbers back to precinct level assignments.

The Elements

To summarize: the most basic element of team policing—geographic stability of assignment—was never realized in New York. The 50% rate of radio runs out of the NPT area by the NPT cars was almost constant.

Communication within the teams varied widely among the different teams, depending on the quality of leadership, but generally the communication was poor. Team commanders were asked to hold frequent team conferences but very few actually did so. This was due partly to difficulties in scheduling a time when the men could all meet and to the strong police antagonism to changing the schedules.

Communication with business interests in the community improved greatly under the NPT program, but there is evidence that NPT officers tended to increase their aggressive tactics towards adolescents and other groups.[4] The teams did not conduct their own series of public meetings for the exchange of information, but they did attend the monthly precinct community council meetings, which were rarely well-attended.

NPT orders suggested that NPT commanders establish liaison with social service agencies, but no adequate referral systems were, in fact, developed. Team commanders did make good use of civilian auxiliaries, assigning them either to independent patrol or patrol with team members.

Unity of supervision was difficult to attain with such large teams (30-35 men) reporting technically to one sergeant, and in actual fact to whichever of many sergeants was on duty. NPT commanders con-

---

[4]See Peter B. Bloch and David I. Specht, *Evaluation Report on Operation Neighborhood: A Rapidly Growing Team Policing Program in New York City* (Washington, D.C.: The Urban Institute, Working Paper No. 4000-3, 1972). This report describes aggressive tactics as including "stop and frisk" and "questioning suspicious individuals." It is unclear, however, whether use of such tactics was seen as responsive or antagonistic to the demands of the community by either the officers employing the tactics, the majority of the community members, or the evaluators.

centrated more on staff supervision and community relations than field command.

The formal and theoretical flexibility of policy-making granted to the team commanders was broader than that given to most of their superiors, but only in rare instances did the commanders use their flexibility.

The patrol and investigative functions were as segregated under the NPT as they had been before. Most NPT areas were served by a plethora of undercover and tactical units, but unified delivery of all services was not a formal intention. In sum, this ambitious effort was well on the way to becoming entrenched, but not in the way it was conceived: NPT is not yet team policing.

Syracuse

Syracuse is not, in terms of problems, a part of the urban crisis. It stands, as the Chamber of Commerce says, "comfortably outside the congestion of the great Eastern megalopolis." It is a college town—Syracuse University is a conspicuous part of the city, but it has had few outbreaks of student militancy. It has three minorities—black, Spanish-speaking and Indian—but they make up only a small percentage of the city. It is a company town of a number of major industries, the most conspicuous of which is General Electric. Its two newspapers are owned and housed together, and they have a supportive attitude toward both the police and General Electric.

The city and county governments are less harmonious. In early 1973, the mayor was still a first-term Democrat, the first in 25 years. The nine-member Common Council was six-to-three Republican, and the registration in Onondaga County was Republican five-to-one. The mayor and the council worked together with difficulty, and the strain was not lessened by a split of responsibilities between the city and the county. The county, headed by a Republican county executive, provided health and welfare services; the city provided, among other things, police services.

The people are prosperous, though not spectacularly so—the "effective buying income per household" in the city is $10,228; in the county, $12,169. Syracuse is surrounded by rather dense suburbs—there are 200,000 city residents and 270,000 suburbanities.

The Department

In early 1973, the Syracuse Police Department was composed of 476 sworn men and women, including eight blacks and one Puerto Rican. The County Civil Service Commission had rigid control of hiring and promotion. The department had been involved in a variety of reorganizations for a decade. In the early 1960's, after a gambling payoff scandal, Patrick V. Murphy, later Police Commissioner of New York, came to Syracuse for 18 months and established a new, firm discipline. He was succeeded by other capable chiefs, also from New York City, William H. T. Smith and John O'Connor. O'Connor was followed by Thomas Sardino, who rose from the department ranks and is a man of striking personality and ability.

34

The waves of reform and reorganization, however, seem to have had an unfortunate side-effect—the engendering of a quiet resistance from the police rank and file. The chiefs and their close advisors had found it increasingly difficult to develop middle management enthusiasm for innovation; the middle management group, firmly fixed in place by civil service, had developed in some cases "this too will pass" attitudes. The latest innovation—team policing—began to take shape in 1968 and the resistance to it began soon after.

The Teams

The Syracuse team project grew out of a combination of circumstances and opportunities rather than a particular community problem. The General Electric Electronics Laboratory, located in Syracuse, wished to apply modern technology to public service in general and crime control in particular. In 1967 a General Electric physicist, Dr. James F. Elliott, received permission from Chief W. H. T. Smith to study the department. The study continued under Chief John O'Connor. Dr. Elliott was one of the first scientists to apply systems analysis to a police department. Elliott and O'Connor sought to use manpower more efficiently to reduce the number of crimes committed and to increase the number of crimes solved. The result of his study was the Crime Control Team (CCT) launched in July of 1968 under the command of then-Lieutenant Thomas Sardino.

The team was designed as the basic unit in a decentralized municipal police force. The team leader, Sardino, had responsibility for controlling crime in his beat, just as the chief had the responsibility for the entire city. The team leader was given almost total flexibility and discretion for how to best use his available resources in day-to-day operations. He reported directly to the chief.

What distinguished the CCT from other team programs was the division of labor between crime and service functions. Initially, the CCT officers were responsible for crime control in their beat, while the regular patrol officers from other beats were called in to handle all non-criminal service functions. The theory was that the Crime Control Team, free from non-crime jobs, would be better able to intercept street crimes in progress. The CCT was supposed to employ three major tactics in crime control—prevention, interception and investigation—and the team leader was responsible for determining which to concentrate on at any given time.

Lieutenant Sardino was given the primary responsibility for setting up the initial team experiment. He interviewed select experienced officers and persuaded eight to volunteer. The eight were assigned responsibility for Area 50, one of Syracuse's 23 beats. These eight officers kept at least one car on the beat 24 hours a day, seven days a week. During high-crime periods, they also routinely deployed an additional one-to-three units.

In theory, the team did not respond to service calls (cats in trees, traffic accidents and such) or calls involving minor crimes (prostitution, gambling, drug abuse). The non-team patrol officers called into the team area to perform only non-crime functions, however, resented handling only non-crime calls; they felt they were being over-burdened with menial chores. Also, the team members felt that the other patrol officers were destroying the good things that the CCT was doing in the neighborhood. Thus, after less than a year, a service unit was made part of the CCT, and the entire area was removed from Patrol Bureau command.

The Neighborhoods

Area 50 was a white working-class area in which many of the Syracuse policemen had been raised. The neighborhood received the team with enthusiasm, and it was an immediate apparent success. The year before the CCT was introduced, Area 50 had had the third highest amount of crime in the city. In the first year of the CCT, crime in the neighborhood was reduced, and the clearance rate was the highest of any beat in the city.[5]

The achievements of the first team were given national publicity by General Electric, and early in 1969 a new team was added in Areas 62 and 63, black and student neighborhoods. In 1971 and again in 1972, more teams were deployed. By early 1973 there were CCT's in seven of the city's 23 beats with a total of 74 team members. Using reported crime rates as a measurement, the teams were successful. In all team areas but one there was a crime reduction. The clearance rate for

---

[5]During the first year of the CCT (mid-1968 to mid-1969), crime fell throughout the city but began increasing again by early 1969. By mid-1969, all crime in Area 50 was 65% of the pre-CCT level and Part I crime was only 53% of its former rate. No other area of the city experienced such a reduction of all crime, and Part I crime for the whole city was up to 73% of its former rate. See *Final Report: Crime Control Team II*, OCCP Proposal No. 433, November 1970 to February 1973, prepared for State of New York Office of Crime Control Planning by Syracuse Police Department (Syracuse, N.Y.: 1973).

the CCT areas was consistently higher (31%) than for the city as a whole (26%).

There is no available data on citizens' attitudes toward the program, but building strong ties between the teams and the neighborhoods was not emphasized at first. The teams worked out of a single suite of offices in the downtown highrise municipal building rather than in neighborhood police stations, and there was little systematic effort to build support. Still the team won a measure of acceptance, and in their first neighborhood, Area 50, the residents continued to supply the team with considerable information.

Some Problems

Dr. Elliott's particular emphasis continued to be on the separation of tasks—"crime" and "service"—but the separation proved more theoretical than practical. Since there is seldom any great glut of calls in Syracuse, it is not surprising that in practice service officers responded to crime calls and crime officers found time to do service tasks. One officer assigned to crime control said that he had spent most of the previous day delivering municipal notices to householders, and he said he routinely spent a good amount of time ticketing illegally parked cars on the Syracuse University campus.

The Syracuse teams did not develop participatory management to any marked degree, but it was not considered an essential element for crime control. Team conferences were held infrequently and were focused not on area problems but on complaints about equipment and other minor matters. The teams never became popular with non-team members—their uniforms differed in one detail, the color of their shirts, and the general patrol referred to them derisively as the "white shirts." When Sardino attempted to find experienced volunteers for his later teams he struck an impasse and then sought to create a new *esprit de corps* by staffing the teams with new recruits and young officers.

Chief Sardino displayed a determined appreciation of the potential of team policing and an awareness of the need to adjust textbook theories to reality. He commented when asked about the results of team policing:

> The original purpose of the experiment was to demonstrate that the CCT organizational concept was a more effective way to control crime. Early in the program the difficulty (if not impossibility) of demonstrating

this premise became obvious.[6] However, it was also obvious that the CCT experiment was serving as a very useful vehicle for introducing and evaluating desirable changes into the Syracuse Police Department, particularly accountability and responsibility: responsibility for geographical areas and accountability by the officers. We want to push accountability down through the department until the patrol officer is fully accountable for what happens on his beat and for the control of crime there.

The Elements

To summarize: The CCT fell short of the three basic elements for team policing. It maintained geographic stability of manpower assignment, but failed to achieve tight communication within the teams. Team conferences were held infrequently and failed to deal with area problems.

Communication with the community seems to have been achieved only in the first CCT area (the white working-class neighborhood) but fell short in black and student areas. This is hardly surprising, given the white working-class background of the policemen. No public meetings were held with the community, although funds were provided for this by a federal grant. None of the teams established solid referral liaisons with other city agencies. Though Area 50 residents did provide the police with much information, there was no other community participation in police work.

Of the three organizational supports, the Syracuse CCT maintained unity of supervision.

Excepting major civil disorders, the team leaders had authority for unified delivery of all services to their areas.

Policy-setting flexibility at the lower level of the hierarchy was theoretically present but did not in fact develop.

The patrol and investigative functions were combined, but the distinction between crime and service cars existed more on paper than in the field.

Thus, the CCT was an ambitious program, more sophisticated in its conception than in its implementation.

---

[6]Perhaps the "difficulty" refers to the fact that crime dropped throughout the city during the first year of the CCT and thus obfuscated the particular effects of the CCT; or perhaps it just recognizes the fact that no one yet understands what combination of variables reduces or "controls" crime.

Holyoke

Holyoke, Massachusetts is a small city on the banks of the Connecticut River. In 1972, it had approximately 50,000 people—its whole population was less than Dayton's Fifth District. Paper mills had once provided employment for most of the residents, but by 1972 the industry had both faded and automated, thus creating employment problems in the city and making a patrolman's job more attractive.

Holyoke, and particularly Ward One, had traditionally been Irish and French-Canadian. By 1972, however, most of the Irish and many of the French residents had moved from the old neighborhoods to the suburbs or to more affluent sections of the city. The Irish still held most of the police ranks above sergeant. The city also had about 5,000 Puerto Ricans, most of whom had arrived in the past few years, and about 1,200 blacks. The old New Englanders who owned the mills and sent their children to the nearby prestigious colleges were an affluent minority.

Holyoke's government was composed of a strong mayor and a Board of Aldermen. In 1972, the city was small but sophisticated.

The Department

In February 1973, the police department had only 117 people, many of whom were related to each other. The chief was appointed and could be dismissed by the mayor. He could be and others had been—Holyoke had had three chiefs in three years. The mayor was a determined advocate of team policing and, not surprisingly, the new chief was also. The chief, Peter F. Kingsley, had been selected to bring administrative order out of chaos. He had served as a part-time park policeman for 23 years while holding a second job as an insurance investigator.

The force was headquartered next to City Hall in an ancient building. It had 93 patrol officers, four captains, six lieutenants, eight sergeants, five detective sergeants, and one radio officer. In the fall of 1972 it was four below its authorized strength of 121, and it had 129 applicants. Its officers had the lowest pay of all police departments in Massachusetts and of all the departments included in this book. A patrol officer received a starting salary of $8,150 a year. He could advance to around $9,000 in three years but would receive no further in-

39

creases unless he was promoted. A great many, possibly a majority, of the men had second jobs. Police officers could retire when 55 years old or when they had had 30 years of service. In late 1972 it was assumed that the force would lose 30% of its members within the next five years through retirement.

The need for change in the department became apparent in late 1969, before Kingsley took over. Police officials met with city and state officials to discuss new police techniques and funding. Representatives of both the Holyoke Model Cities Agency and the Massachusetts Governor's office played significant roles, arguing that a stand-off existed between the police and the city's Puerto Rican community in Ward One. They felt that the community saw the police as brutal men with clubs, and that the police saw the community as tempestuous people with no respect for law and order. A demand for police change was the inevitable outcome of the discussions, but the department was allowed to determine for itself the form of change that would best suit the needs of both the police and the community.

The team policing experiment began in December 1970, with a $40,000 grant from the U.S. Justice Department's Law Enforcement Assistance Administration and a $100,000 grant from Model Cities. The top echelons were reported enthusiastic, but many of the rank and file were not. As Chief Kingsley said later, "The idea of change doesn't appeal to most of them."

The Neighborhood

Ward One, "The Flats," curved into the Connecticut River and was separated from the rest of the town by overpasses and railroad tracks. It was old and crowded, with 5,000 people in 23 city blocks. It had almost all of the city's Puerto Ricans, much of its poverty and most of its crime. The city's few blacks lived along the river, too, but most of them were in adjacent Ward Two. In the summer of 1970, Ward One had had open racial conflict, which badly frightened the residents and neighborhood merchants.

The Team

The team went into Ward One in December 1970. Its primary objectives were to reduce crime, bring ethnic peace to the Ward and still the fears of its merchants. Captain George F. Burns, Jr. was in charge of 12 police officers and 4 Community Service Officers. The latter were Puerto Ricans. The team provided all police services for Ward One except homicide investigations. It worked out of a ground-floor office in an apartment building, with signs outside in Spanish. All area calls either came directly to the team office or were immediately transferred there from headquarters. Usually working in blue blazers and gray slacks rather than in regular police uniforms, the team entertained a constant flow of visitors of all ages both in the storefront office and out on patrol. It was headed by the captain, but the patrolmen elected a chairman from among their ranks and formed committees to study specific problems. Team members set policy, made schedules, and distributed the workload. Captain Burns reported directly to the mayor.

By some simple measures it was a quick success. The team received 90 calls in its first month—76 more than were usual for Ward One—a fact which was interpreted as a sign of increasing community confidence in the police. The First Ward Alderman made a personal tour of the area and reported that he had found no one who did not feel that the team had been an improvement.

On a cold night during the first week of the team's operation, the apartment building in which the team had its headquarters caught fire. The officers roused the residents and got them out without loss of life. They then, after great efforts, provided Christmas presents and dinners for those burned out. The team's response to the tragedy had a significant, positive effect on their relationship to the residents of The Flats.

The team later moved into a storefront adjoining a restaurant and then, toward the end of the year, into the basement of the new Model Cities building. This latter move served to illustrate the fact that, in Holyoke at least, the storefront approach to the neighborhood had positive significance. In the Model Cities building, calls and visits dropped spectacularly. To get to the team's new and handsome quarters, a visitor had to enter an austere building and find his way down the stairs and corridors. Few made the trip. The team then decided to move again, and obtained an empty corner store. The team members cleaned and painted the quarters, put up Spanish signs outside, and moved in. The number of visitors increased immediately.

The First Ward team had some success and some problems. By early 1973 the merchants' initial fear had abated but not disappeared. Stores that had curtailed their hours to avoid after-school crowds of

Puerto Rican boys had not gone back to the old hours of opening and closing. Nevertheless, the team accomplishments had been noteworthy. The storefront received regular drop-in visits from its Puerto Rican neighbors and, perhaps most notably, its corner had become a routine gathering place for teen-age boys. They were not ostentatiously friendly to the police, but they said "hello" to them as they passed. Many of the buildings in the area were decorated with graffiti and slogans calling for Puerto Rican independence, but no one had written anything about the police, offensive or otherwise, on their building or on any building observed.

In 1973 the team program was being extended to other sections of Holyoke, and it was the chief's announced intention to make it city-wide. It was not certain, however, that the expansion would be as successful as the first attempt, since the first team's members had been volunteers and thus had brought with them a natural enthusiasm. There was resistance to the program within the police department, which took the form of apathy or irritation rather than of outright opposition or sabotage. The force was being systematically trained for team duty and, according to Captain Burns, the training sessions mirrored the resistance. During a one-hour session which Burns was conducting, there were nine men in the class—all over 30 and four over 40. About half of the men present asked questions or made comments which were more or less hostile to the idea of team policing. Still team policing, at least in its first stages, had accomplished a great deal.

The second team went into operation in the fall of 1972 in Ward Two, the river section adjacent to Ward One. At the insistence of the Ward Two Alderman and the residents, the team wore standard police uniforms (though the chief said he intended to give them at least an identifying color or stripe on their hats). Instead of a storefront, they were housed in a former convent, where they were hardly visible and rarely visited. This divergence from blazers and storefronts was not necessarily bad, however. Teams were intended to reflect their neighborhoods, and Ward Two had different needs from Ward One. The population was less dense, more middle class, and required less active police service.

There was opposition to the Holyoke team experiment, the nature of which was probably not much different than the opposition found in Dayton. But the Holyoke team did have an easier time. Holyoke was a smaller department—117 officers instead of 400. Everything was on a more personal basis. The ethnic hostility in Holyoke also was on a smaller scale than Dayton's—the numbers were smaller and the violence circumscribed. In addition, Holyoke had strong leadership: the mayor was determined to see that the project succeeded, and he had direct control of the department.

The "success" of Holyoke's team policing program, as defined by the response of the community, became a problem as the project developed. The question of who should get the credit for the success provoked a number of personality clashes. The rest of the police department grew to resent the publicity which the team policing unit received; therefore, when the time came to expand the program—with the ready support of federal funding agencies—the political situation in Holyoke was so volatile that the future prospects of team policing in the city seemed bleak. Nonetheless, the team concept eventually won out, and will be extended throughout the city.[7]

The Elements

In Holyoke all three operational elements of team policing were achieved. The geographic stability of the team was virtually absolute. In no cases did other patrolmen come into or team members go out of the team area.

Maximum interaction among the officers was achieved, primarily due to the small size of the team and the nature of its area, which facilitated informal exchange of information. Formal communication was practiced in weekly policy-setting meetings attended by the entire team, in which major problems were brought to the attention of the group and discussed. Problems and issues were directed to the attention of team committees for consideration and recommendations for a team decision.

Communication among the members of the teams and members of the community was great, on both an informal and formal level. Public meetings were held monthly to review problems and to help define policy needs and directions. These were well attended and allowed considerable community input. The community also participated in police work by supplying much information to the team.

---

[7]See Helen Campbell O'Malley, *Evaluation Report on the Holyoke Team Police Experiment of the Holyoke Police Department* (Holyoke, Mass.: Holyoke Police Department, June 1973).

The four organizational supports were also met, for the most part, in the Holyoke project. Unity of supervision was maintained under the team captain. Flexibility of the team's policy-making authority was virtually absolute and well used. The team even wrote its own manual of rules and procedures.

Moreover, the teams provided unified delivery of services, taking total authority for their areas (except for homicides). In fact, the team did not allow any non-team patrolmen to enter The Flats even on official business. The team had combined responsibility for both patrol and investigative functions. The consistency of the relationship of the team to the community was therefore absolute.

Los Angeles

The City of Los Angeles is, in lifestyles and geographic spread, a composite of dozens of little cities—connected by freeways but separated by economic and cultural disparities. The 1970 population was 2,816,000; 17.9% was black and 18.4% was Spanish-speaking or of Spanish surname. Median family income for the city was $10,602, while for black families it was $7,198 and for Spanish families it was $8,240. Less than 10% of the city's families had incomes below poverty level, compared with over 21% of black families and 15% of Spanish families.

Economic and ethnic differences are exaggerated by the separateness and homogeneity of each community. Unlike New York City, where diversity is spread throughout the city, Los Angeles has distinct communities with little communication between them and thus considerable suspicion and hostility from one to another.

The Department

The Los Angeles Police Department has been known as a highly centralized, efficient and impersonal organization. In the 1950's, Chief William Parker, a man of outstanding ability and integrity, had shaped it into the model suggested by O. W. Wilson. By the early Sixties, it appeared to be the ideal centralized professional police department. By the late Sixties, however, explosive incidents such as the Watts riots led police officials to conclude that centralization was not the most effective organizational style for providing satisfactory police services in the many diverse neighborhoods of Los Angeles.

In November 1969, Chief Edward M. Davis moved toward "community mobilization" with his Basic Car Plan, a limited form of team policing. It began on an experimental basis in Los Angeles' Hollywood section, which includes a range of neighborhoods from glamorous to run-down. Several months later, the members of the Los Angeles City Council, who were painfully aware of the political pressures of urban crime, saw the Basic Car Plan as at least a partial solution to the problems and they demanded that it be extended at once. Although it was still an untested system, it was adopted city-wide.

Under the Basic Car Plan, a patrol car was permanently assigned

45

to a neighborhood. The officers assigned to that car tried to build community support by frequent appearances at public gatherings, where they presented prepared programs. They did not attempt to convert militant anti-police factions but tried to mobilize the other citizens in the communities. The plan was only a limited success. It proved difficult for the dispatchers to keep the Basic Cars in their assigned neighborhoods, even when they were supported by non-team cars, which were supposed to operate across neighborhood boundaries. Also, the efforts at community contact retained the former impersonal department style—the neighborhood police were lecturers on high school auditorium stages, not neighborhood officers chatting with neighborhood residents.

But all along the department was refining the basic idea. Captain Robert Vernon (later Commander), who was in charge of the Venice Division, suggested a much more complex version of team policing. Chief Davis told him to submit his concept to the Department Crime Control Committee. The Committee approved it and asked the California Council of Criminal Justice (CCCJ)[8] for funding. The CCCJ was particularly interested in anti-burglary proposals, so while the plan was originally conceived as a broad, all-inclusive team policing effort, it was offered as a specific burglary control strategy. For this reason a section of the Venice Division, where the residents were particularly alarmed by the rise in burglaries, was chosen as the proposed team site—the beat patrolled by a single Basic Car. This effort was followed by further systematic moves toward the decentralization of the department.

The Neighborhood

Los Angeles is divided for police purposes into 17 Divisions. The Divisions are subdivided into Districts. Venice is a Division with six Districts and a population of 180,000. In 1972, it was described by police as a "microcosm of Los Angeles," with several distinct socioeconomic communities. In the spring of 1972, team policing was introduced into one District of Venice previously served by Basic Car 28. It included the neighborhoods of Palms, Mar Vista and Westdale, and had 35,000 citizens living in three square miles. It was an affluent homogeneous community. Ninety-five percent of its residents were

---

[8]The LEAA State Planning Agency.

46

white, 3% Spanish-speaking and 2% black or Oriental. Most people owned their own homes and had become concerned with the increasing prevalence of burglars.

The team experiment in Venice, conceived as an extension of the Basic Car Plan, was financed by a $259,000 grant from the California Council of Criminal Justice, which was in turn supported by the federal Law Enforcement Assistance Administration. TEAM became its acronym (Team Experiment in Area Mobilization) and its focus was uniquely clear—it was designed to reduce crime, but its immediate goal was to reduce burglaries. In selecting the District, the planners weighed several factors: the number of burglaries in recent years, the number and types of old and new homes, the number of multiple dwellings and businesses, and get-away access to freeways. The intention was to choose a typical—not an exaggerated—laboratory for testing the team.

The Team

The team had responsibility for one-sixth of the Venice Division and had roughly one-sixth of the Division's manpower and equipment. A lieutenant II, rather than a sergeant, was in charge. The officers were not actual volunteers: they were deliberately chosen to reflect the various levels of competence within the department. Once chosen, however, they could decline the invitation. The ratings of the officers finally selected were proportionate to those in the department as a whole. The intention was to test the team idea as scientifically as possible. It began with 39 men and two women.[9]

The beginning was carefully planned. There was a three-day organizational development seminar, a "retreat" at the Forest Home Christian Conference Center. The Center was selected for its atmosphere of calm and meditation. The group went there in police buses and stayed together night and day. Senior officers roomed with probationary officers. Community relations experts were paired with officers known to have somewhat anti-community relations attitudes. The group was given attitudinal tests at the beginning and again at the end of the seminar. They were tested a third time after six months as team members.

---

[9]One lieutenant II, 1 sergeant II, 3 sergeants I, 22 patrol policemen, 3 traffic enforcement policemen, 2 accident investigation policemen, 1 administrative assistant, 2 clerk-typists, 2 investigators I, 2 investigators II, 1 policeman III-investigator. The women's duties were entirely clerical.

The goal of the seminar was to involve the future participants in the planning of the team—in "participatory management." The seminar had a precise sequence: (1) to establish team objectives; (2) to complete organizational plans; (3) to establish deployment and watch hours; (4) to set community involvement goals; (5) to determine equipment needs; (6) to delineate jurisdictional and dispatching policies; and (7) to define patrol, traffic, and investigative functions. Certain limitations were set, however. The participants could not change the Los Angeles Police Department uniform, salary structure, or discipline techniques. And all plans and schemes adopted had to be "legal, ethical, and moral."

The most critical and uncomfortable session was the opening one. Captain Vernon told the officers why and how they had been selected and the reasons for the team experiment. He announced that during the seminar all ranks would be ignored and that any person who addressed another by rank would be fined ten cents. Dinner seating arrangements were changed at each meal to break up the old cliques (traffic, investigators, etc.) and to prevent new ones from forming. The officers were advised that each could interrupt any discussion by shouting "process" when he felt that the discussion was straying from the point. Everyone would then vote on whether the shouter's point was well taken and whether they should get back to fundamentals or continue in the same direction. Together the members of the new team decided that they would work three watches, with overlap; that they would have six marked police cars and four unmarked cars; that no team cars would be sent out of the area except in an emergency; that no outside cars would come in except in an emergency; that the traffic officers would continue to take a primary interest in traffic but would function more as generalists; and that investigators would be deployed by area.

When the seminar began, the planners were pessimistic. They considered it unlikely that the officers from the various sections—traffic, patrol, etc.—would be "willing to accept the new freedom and be able to work together and share responsibility." At the end of the seminar, however, the investigators (the detectives) announced "in all sincerity" that they would do everything in their power to train the other team members in investigative techniques and to see that the team functioned effectively as a whole. The traffic officers decided on their own to abandon their distinctive white helmets. Team members also offered

48

specific suggestions for achieving various goals—they would recruit "block captains" among area residents and they would try "tandem car" policing and bike patrols.

Team 28's most notable achievement may have been its continued flexibility. A technique once adopted did not become sanctified—strategies could be abandoned if they did not work. The team adopted "tandem" and "parallel" patrolling shortly after it was formed. Cars in "tandem" worked in pairs, one two blocks behind the other, and each car with one officer. Cars in "parallel" worked side by side, one block apart. In theory the two officers would have greater mobility than if both were in the same car. In practice they found that they were so constantly concerned with keeping track of each other that they had less time to simply watch for law violations. There was also a lessened sense of security when an officer answered a call alone (even if his partner was supposedly only two blocks away and answering, too). For a while the team experimented with having both officers acknowledge every call, but that tied up the dispatcher. So tandem and parallel patrolling were put aside.

On the other hand, the team scored a great success in stake-outs. The neighborhood was the target of a particularly industrious cat burglar who disappeared from the streets before the police could arrive. The team staked out a dozen men—using various disguises and hand radios—in the areas of the burglaries. They caught the burglar on the first day. (Because he lived in the neighborhood, he had been able to disappear rapidly after each job.) Using the same technique, the team subsequently caught two other cat burglars. The officers attributed their success to the fact that as a team they were used to working together and to the fact that they knew every alley and cut-through in the neighborhood.

Although the cat burglary caper was in itself statistically insignificant, it made a marked impression on the residents and possibly on potential burglars.[10] On one occasion when team members stopped a carload of suspicious young men, the latter explained that they had not realized that they were in Team 28's territory and they promised to leave it immediately.

---

[10]The department considered the overall anti-burglary effort spectacularly successful. It reported that burglaries were reduced by almost 50% during the first six months of team operation. Even in the first month, the reduction was 40%, and it was maintained and improved in each subsequent month.

The enthusiasm of the team members was reflected in the Block Captain Program. One hundred fifty block captains were recruited in the first month and another 150 by the fall. Block captains were residents who agreed to maintain a regular liaison with police. They were recruited after they had shown an initial, positive interest in supporting the police, either by visiting the Police Community Center (a storefront featuring educational exhibits)[11] or through casual conversations with patrolling officers. The success of the program was notable. The team members held frequent meetings with the people of a particular block at the block captain's home. One observed meeting was attended by 27 people and another by 21. Eager to talk to the police both about their fears and about solutions to problems, the attendants were middle-aged or elderly, homeowners, married couples and widows.

Twenty-one neighborhood meetings—called "coffee klatches" (sic)—were held in the team's first month and the pace was maintained. By fall, over 12,000 of the 35,000 area residents had had some personal, friendly contact with the team. A police fair which was held in late July at Palms-Mar Vista Park attracted 3,500 people. Some 700 visited the Community Center. At the Center and at the fair, antiburglary locks and alarms were displayed. The fair also featured karate exhibitions, informative lectures, and varieties of entertainment. Some 4,500 residents attended special events such as picnics; 1,250 came to school meetings; and 2,500 attended the neighborhood meetings. No doubt some of the 12,000 total were repeaters, but the achievement was still extraordinary. When one includes the thousands who recognized the team members simply from seeing them on patrol, it appears that a majority of the people in the Team 28 area actually knew their neighborhood cops. The positive response was emphasized by the numerous letters received by the team.[12]

---

[11] The Community Center attracted 285 visitors in August but only 85 in the first half of September. The Center hours were then changed from noon to 8 p.m. to 4 p.m. to 9 p.m. Business increased but not spectacularly, and the team planned to use the Center for "events" rather than simply as a standing exhibit. The Center was eventually closed, however, due to a lack of sustained interest.

[12] The letters were unanimously praising and often emotional: "the rapport between the citizenry with the police department has never been better"; "a definite improvement in feelings of teenagers toward the police"; "I live alone. I actually feel safe with them around"; "It had a great effect on me to see a car marked Team 28 some distance from our home and to know they are doing their best"; "(The team members) are friendly, patient, well-trained and above all, dedicated"; "For the first time in over eight years we are aware of police cars in our neighborhood. The children are delighted when the cars go by."

Team 28 was excellently managed by a lieutenant and five sector sergeants. As "managers," they successfully encouraged and fomented participatory management among the team members. The officers communicated effectively—among themselves and with the community.

The team achieved a number of goals envisioned in the team policing concept. First, it functioned to a great degree as if it were a separate small police department and the lieutenant were the chief of police. (He related to the chief of patrol through the captain of the Venice Division.)

Second, the team members had a clear supportive relationship among themselves. Communication among team members was a major problem in many departments, but for Team 28 the flow of information was smooth. The six plainclothes investigators, for example, shared a long table in the middle of the largest room at the team headquarters. Each man had his folder of current cases, and it remained on the table whether or not he was there. Team members were free to check the folders to see what developments had occurred in cases in which they were interested. The investigators shared with the other team members a file cabinet containing "intelligence" information on known criminals, and all officers were encouraged to contribute.

Third, the training was, in a sense, continuous. At the beginning, and again at six-month intervals, each officer was required to write his understanding of individual and team responsibilities, his six-month goals for himself and the team, and an evaluation of both the system in general and the team's specific progress. At the end of Team 28's first six months, only three out of 37 officers expressed a desire for another assignment. In January 1973, the team had another three-day seminar.

Fourth, as mentioned, the rapport which was developed between the team and the community was exceptional. Although building rapport in a predominantly white and middle-class community is undoubtedly different and perhaps easier than establishing it in a community such as Watts, the planners and managers of TEAM had considered the theoretical implications of team policing beyond the characteristics of this first community. They believed the essential aspect of team work was the ability of the team to consider the particular problems (such as race, crime, socioeconomic attitudes, etc.) of a particular community with a fresh view—to avoid adopting some tactic or technique merely because it had worked elsewhere or because it had been recommended in a manual. For instance, in Venice the most prevalent crime was burglary and the most significant community issue was fear of burglars. The team members, therefore, conducted systematic "Home Security Inspections" to assist the residents in preventing burglaries and held frequent "coffee klatches" to discuss neighborhood problems. "I believe team policing can work anywhere, but in each community it will be different," the lieutenant said. The belief was to be tested.

In early 1973, the department planned to establish three more teams, including one in the 77th Street Division which includes Watts. Commander Vernon said that the department felt that if it worked in the Watts area, team policing would work anywhere, and added, "We do not expect it to be any less a success than Team 28."

Not all the results of the Team 28 experiment were positive, but the team leadership was apparently willing to face the negative as well as the positive aspects. For instance, not all team members were able to adjust to the new style of organization—some performed better than they had under the former system and others who had formerly had top performance ratings were uncomfortable in their new role. One team assessment of its own performance noted that "the burden of responsibility has often weighed heavy on the shoulders of individual policemen. Officers who heretofore were only expected to write tickets or arrest criminals have been saddled with a larger task, forced often unwillingly to be all things to all men—speechmakers, public relations representatives, social worker, psychologist, program planner, writer, researcher, and the enforcer of the law." Inevitably, the readjustment of role required by team policing caused some problems both for some team members and thus for the team as a whole.

Another problem that developed was the pressure and fatigue created by extreme demands on the officers' time. With the extensive participation in "community mobilization" that occurred in Venice, the 35 officers found that they used much of their spare time and energy in serving the 35,000 residents. The team members appeared at the "coffee klatches" and conducted intensive "Home Security Inspections" on the weekends. After the first few months of the program, however, when the pressures were noted, overtime activities were reduced.

In early 1973, the future of Venice-style team policing in Los Angeles seemed bright. The dispatcher problem which had plagued the

Basic Car Plan was not of great concern for Team 28. At one point Team 28 averaged 200 calls (or about 20%) out of their neighborhood, but they still handled 90% of the calls inside their boundaries. Subsequently, the first percentage dropped to about 15% and the second rose. Also, there was little apparent resistance to team policing within the department. In 1973, the concept was being extended and teams were about to be instituted in the Foothill Division located within the San Fernando Valley, the Hollenbeck Division in East Los Angeles, and the 77th Street Division in the southern portion of the city that includes Watts.

The Elements

To summarize: The three basic elements—geographic stability, maximum interaction among the officers, and maximum communication with the community—were all achieved in Venice.

Maximum interaction within the team was accomplished by bringing the officers together frequently to discuss and plan tactics and by encouraging constant exchange of information.

Maximum communication with the community was maintained in day-to-day field operations, as well as in the special meetings and home visits. Referral systems were not used, but liaison with social service agencies was not a goal of the program.

As for the four organizational supports: there was 24-hour a day unity of supervision. A different sergeant commanded the team area on every shift, but one lieutenant had overall responsibility. Because of the limitations on uniforms, the team was not given as much flexibility in policy-making as teams in some other cities had, but the Venice team did make good use of the increased flexibility they were given in other matters. The team's responsibility for its area included unified delivery of all police services.

Richmond

Richmond is sixteen miles northeast of San Francisco and eight miles from the University of California at Berkeley and has a population of 80,000. Incorporated in 1905, its population was still only 23,000 by 1940. During the war, however, many workers came to the new shipyards on San Francisco and San Pablo Bays, and by 1944 Richmond had 100,000 people. It dwindled somewhat after that. By 1973, its population was 40% black, 10% Spanish-speaking, and included many groups with diverse lifestyles.

Richmond looks prosperous—with a new $4 million civic center, Standard Oil's largest refinery in the West, and many attractive homes and parks—and has an excellent police force, but it is troubled by crime. In 1971, it had a crime index rate (number of serious crimes per 100,000 population) of 7,065—more than double both the national average and the average for all cities of population 50,000 to 100,000.

The Department and the Team

The Richmond Police Department, with 156 officers, is headquartered in the modern Hall of Justice building in the Civic Center complex. The public enters a lobby and is faced with a transparent plexiglass wall which shields the police behind the counter. Visitors wishing to call on someone behind the barrier identify themselves first and are then admitted by a pressed buzzer which opens a locked door. The glass wall is not merely a symbolic barrier, however, for gangs have invaded the lobby in times past.

The department is headed by Chief Lourn Phelps, a veteran of the force with a Master's Degree in Criminology from the University of California. He adds distinction to a force that is already unique. Rather recently Richmond had the highest paid patrol officers in the country, and in 1973 they were still among the leaders. Despite the high wage, however, Richmond has had some difficulty in recruiting. The Richmond applicants are rigorously screened and then put on an 18-month probationary period. Generally, from 40 to 60% are eliminated before they pass the final test. It is noteworthy that the average patrol officer is in his mid-twenties.

In June 1968, after much research on different kinds of patrol allocation, Richmond instituted team policing as the most efficient means of improving manpower deployment—not enough officers had been available during peak crime hours, and during slack periods the officers on patrol had not had enough to do. It was also seen as a method of tightening the first-line supervision of patrol officers, for under the traditional system, patrol officers had often been supervised by more than one sergeant and a sergeant sometimes had been responsible for as many as 25 officers. Richmond's program was derived from the model developed in Aberdeen, Scotland in 1947 and first tried in the United States in Tucson, Arizona.

In Richmond team policing, all patrol officers were team members. There were originally 10 teams and the whole city was the neighborhood. Each team had a sergeant and eight to twelve officers who always worked together.[13] Although Richmond teams did not have fixed neighborhoods, each team was unified by time and a close working relationship among the sergeant and the officers. During the quietest hours of the day, a single team might cover the whole city, while during the high-crime hours four teams might overlap. The teams were trained as units under a continuing in-service training system.

Under the team plan the patrol force was organized into five basic teams to cover the 24-hour working day, two relief teams to work days when other teams were off, and a vacation team to relieve teams taking vacations. In March 1972, two additional teams were added as special crime-fighting units. Working closely with the Criminal Investigation Division, these two teams were to work in those areas of the city that might have special crime problems such as burglaries. The Richmond teams differed from all others observed in that they did not have separate neighborhoods. Chief Phelps explained: "Some people use team policing as a geographic concept. . . . A more appropriate use. . . would be to denote a functional entity—a working team—and this is the meaning of team policing . . . for the Richmond Police Department."[14]

Chief Phelps believed the program had been well accepted by the patrol officers because the change had been made with the deliberate

---

[13]As of April 1973, Richmond had 13 teams, each with five to seven patrol officers—eight basic teams, four relief teams, and one specialty team. Five teams overlap during peak crime hours on Friday and Saturday nights.

[14]"Team Policing—Four Years Later," by Lourn G. Phelps and Sgt. Lorne Harmon, *FBI Law Enforcement Bulletin,* December 1972.

inclusion of incentives. Careful planning had made it possible for 60% of the team members to have either Saturday or Sunday off each week. This was a more satisfactory arrangement than had been possible during the watch system. It was also possible to let each team arrange its own vacation schedule, so that almost everyone had time off during the summer.

In addition, the more routine and time-consuming tasks, such as directing traffic and writing misdemeanor reports, were given to the Community Service Officers. Six of the teams each had one CSO. The CSO's wore uniforms but did not carry weapons or make arrests.

Each team held meetings twice weekly to discuss plans and tactics. Teams sometimes wore civilian clothes, rode bikes, and had either one, two, three or four officers in a car.

Team policing changed the role of the sergeant and his relationship to his officers. Under the new organization, sergeants had responsibility for only eight to twelve officers and worked the same hours and days as their officers; therefore, they soon got to know the strengths and weaknesses of each. Each team tended to adopt the personality and style of its sergeant and thus develop its own identity. The distinct team styles were reinforced by the practice of conducting in-service training for the team as a unit, including the sergeant. Thus, when the entire force was given special family crisis intervention training, the training was given separately to each team. The trainer noted that each team tended to approach the problem with enthusiasm or skepticism depending largely upon the sergeant's attitude. One problem which resulted from the strengthening of the sergeant's role was some confusion as to the role of the lieutenants. The lieutenants, as of early 1972, were still working watches and their shifts consequently overlapped team shifts—in effect, a team worked for more than one lieutenant.

The team members had considerably more investigative responsibility than they had had under the watch system—they sometimes followed cases up to the signing of complaints, although the Detective Bureau still functioned independently of the teams. Chief Phelps planned, however, to make detectives, as well as community relations officers and other specialists, part of the teams.

The teams developed a high level of cooperation, as evidenced by the ingenious removal of 25 local Indians who occupied a NIKE base. The department was under considerable pressure from the army to remove the Indians immediately and forceably. The department's considered goal, however, was to persuade the Indians to leave with a minimum use of force and to avoid appearing to the general public or the Indians as a harassing force. The department gave the impression that they planned no action at all. Then the entire force was assembled quietly one evening, and tactics were discussed. The combined teams, with the cooperation of the Contra Costa County Sheriff's Department, East Bay Regional Park Police, and the United States 6th Army, moved to the NIKE base at 5:30 a.m. when all the occupying Indians were asleep. The officers worked with their own team mates but in cooperation with all others, and provided leadership to the personnel of the other agencies. Only a few leaders of the Indians were to be arrested and each arrest was to be made by a specific team. Those arrested were taken to a high school cafeteria and then released without charges. It was correctly assumed that the remaining Indians would follow, so buses were provided to take them to the cafeteria also.

Phelps considered his teams a success, but not an unqualified one: "It is clear that team policing is a mixed benefit. It solves some traditional problems, but creates some new ones .... In general, team policing is seen as a distinct improvement by most Richmond Police Department personnel, although there are a few officers who express a preference for the old system."[15]

The Elements

To summarize: Richmond developed a "time team," not an area team like the others in the study. Its central element was interaction among team members, and that was implemented very well. The organizational supports for achieving that element were also present: unity of supervision, low-level flexibility, and combined patrol-investigative functions in the team. Unified delivery of services was not a requirement of the program, since the teams were not area-based. Thus, while it was not as ambitious a project as the others, it certainly succeeded in meeting its goals.

---

[15]"Team Policing —Four Years Later," *op. cit.*

Chapter III
Preparation for Team Policing: Goals, Plans and Training

The first and in some ways the most important step in implementing a team program is the setting of objectives and goals of the program. Team policing projects generally have one broad public goal—to improve the control of crime through better community relations and more effective police organization.

In Detroit, for example, the goal of the team program was to:

> ... improve police-community relations. In addition, we hope to achieve the even more important goal of reducing crime. Crime-control may result directly from referral and action programs. Crime-control also may result because the police are permanently assigned to a neighborhood and will be better known to the community. If police are better known by the community and increase the service which they give, they may find people more willing to cooperate with them in reporting serious crimes and undergoing the inconvenience of giving testimony.[16]

The Los Angeles Basic Car Plan and the Dayton Team Program both were specifically aimed at gaining the support of the people being policed. In Los Angeles, the Basic Car Plan attempted to:

> ... develop a sense of personal responsibility in police officers for the persons and property in an assigned area, increase the ability to anticipate crime and react to calls, and improve communication and cooperation between police and the community through regular contact. If it achieves these objectives, the Basic Car concept represents a major approach to the problems of crime and disorder facing society.[17]

---

[16]Evaluation grant application to the Ford Foundation submitted by the Urban Institute.
[17]Commander Robert Vernon, personal document.

61

In Dayton, the stated premises were:

> Policing cannot be successful without the support of the people in the
> neighborhood being policed. And this support will not appear unless the
> police working in that area are responsive to the residents of the neighbor-
> hood. It is no easy task for a police organization to become responsive to
> neighborhood concerns, often punctuated with severe conflict. The suc-
> cess of the police existence will depend on development of a satisfactory
> role by the police; a role that can allow for neighborhood responsiveness
> while maintaining community respect. If crime is of concern to a neigh-
> borhood, so are the methods utilized by police departments to combat that
> crime. While placement of a police officer on every street corner may
> drastically reduce street crime, it is neither economically nor politically
> acceptable to do so if for no other reason than the result would be an
> army of occupation in a democratic society.
>
> Through the team policing program, the Dayton Police Department in-
> tends to accomplish three major goals:
>
> (1) Test the effectiveness of a generalist approach to police service as
> opposed to the specialist approach now utilized by all major police or-
> ganizations.
>
> (2) Produce a community-centered police structure that is responsive
> to neighborhood concerns and understanding of neighborhood life-styles,
> and
>
> (3) Alter the bureaucratic structure of the police organization away
> from the militaristic model toward a neighborhood oriented professional
> model.
>
> The overall goal, of course, . . . to provide effective police service to a
> neighborhood while establishing a positive relationship between neighbor-
> hood residents and the police.[18]

Programs often had unannounced objectives. Police Commissioner Patrick V. Murphy, when he was in Detroit, was primarily concerned with bridging the gap between the police and a hostile community; when he instituted team policing in New York, he was also extremely anxious to increase the productivity of the patrol officer, to
get patrol officers to answer the radio when the dispatcher called, and
to report back to the dispatcher as soon as the radio call had been
completed.

Who Does the Planning?

The support or resistance of the non-team members was probably
the most critical factor in determining the degree of success of team

---

[18]Grant application to the National Institute of Law Enforcement and Criminal Justice.

policing. It is clear from the case studies that in those cities where members of the department—the command officers, the middle management and patrol officers—were involved in the planning and training, the team programs were more effective. They were involved as soon as possible, and they were actively involved. The goals were articulated within the department, but there was also a role in goal-setting for outsiders. In most of the cities studied, outsiders—sociologists, lawyers, scientists—were active in initial planning, notably in Holyoke, Dayton, Syracuse and, to a lesser degree, in New York. In Syracuse, the General Electric Electronics Laboratory loaned a top physicist to the police department for a year, during which time he suggested and then helped plan the Crime Control Team. In Dayton, a civilian assistant to Chief Robert Igleburger developed the theory of abolishing the hierarchical police structure and adopting a generalist-specialist model of patrol.

Where the civilian planners dominated, however, there were unfortunate side effects. The top- and middle-uniformed officers of the police departments were usually by-passed in the process. The civilians were frequently engaging in their first working experience within a police department and tended to talk only to the chiefs. The chiefs, in turn, welcomed an opportunity to discuss police problems with these sophisticated outsiders. Neither the chiefs nor the newcomers saw the need to involve other police officials. This closed planning process was encouraged by its apparent efficiency. The goal-setting process was usually tied to preparing applications for federal funding, and obtaining funds was perceived as a job for the chief and civilian experts. The intention was to involve lower officials once the money was in.

By the time the funds arrived, however, the shape of the project had jelled. Even then the chief often assigned the civilian planner to explain the project to department personnel. For example, after Commissioner Murphy received a $150,000 Ford Foundation grant for Peter Bloch of the Urban Institute to evaluate the Beat Commander project in Detroit, he circulated among his command staff the grant proposal and a Murphy-Bloch article in *Police Chief,* a publication of the International Association of Chiefs of Police. The project was then discussed at a staff meeting, and Bloch prepared guidelines for the staff's comment. Bloch then met individually with command staff members and rewrote the guidelines in response to their criticism. This process did not work. The command staff still felt that they had been left out of the planning. And as we noted earlier, the project, though a success in terms of its own accomplishments, was resisted by most of the department, and after Murphy left Detroit it was dropped.

In most cities, rank and file found out about the team policing plan when it was announced in the press, a *fait accompli.* In Dayton, where line police were largely left out of the planning, the Fraternal Order of Police became very much involved—as opponents, not supporters. However, New York did involve its patrolman's union—the strongest in the country—in the planning discussions of the Neighborhood Police Team project. Consequently there has been little or no organized resistance to team policing in New York. The union leaders were agreeable as long as their members did not complain. Holyoke, Massachusetts and Venice, California also involved rank-and-file officers in substantive program planning.

In Holyoke, after the team members were selected, the outside consultants then made it clear that the patrol officers, not the consultants, were responsible for developing the experiment. The consultants limited their own role to suggesting options and furnishing specific information. In this case, planning became training, although it was not labeled as such. Subcommittees of patrol officers were formed on such matters as uniforms, equipment, how to perform an investigation, and the rules and procedures for the team. Once the officers were convinced that the program was their own, they took the initiative. They made some quick decisions on equipment by contacting vendors directly. The decision to wear blazers was reached after the uniform subcommittee had arranged for fashion-show presentations. Another subcommittee developed a new team policy and procedures manual, which spelled out its policy-making process and the functions of the team chairman and various committees.

In the Los Angeles-Venice team, the prospective team members shaped the specifics of the program at a three-day around-the-clock workshop, in which the heavy stress was on their participatory management—both at the seminar and eventually in the field.

Selecting the Site

In the cities studied, the target areas were chosen by the chiefs and their advisors, usually civilians, before the teams were operational. Ward One was chosen in Holyoke because that was where the violence was. Los Angeles chose the neighborhood in Venice because citizens there were acutely concerned with burglaries, and the team was formally conceived as an anti-burglary operation.

In Syracuse, the team program began in a stable, white neighborhood, which had the third highest amount of crime in the city the year before. But it was, by tradition, apt to be naturally pro-police. The reasoning was to give the demonstration project an optimum chance of success—a strategy which paid off, since the program was immediately popular.

In Detroit and New York, the need to show concern for the problems of black ghetto areas demanded that such areas be the focus for innovation. Thus, the highest crime sector of the highest crime precinct in Detroit was selected, and Brooklyn's high-crime Bedford-Stuyvesant area was chosen in New York. When the program was expanded to less crime-ridden precincts, the areas chosen were always those with the highest crime rates in the precinct. Utilization of crime rate as the criterion for area selection was also a political device. Given the popularity of the program in New York where communities often saw team policing as a means of increasing manpower in the area, the crime rate was the only way to justify selecting one part of a precinct over another.

The most successful team sites were ones in which the team could function as a separate unit. When a unit (e.g., a precinct) was part team and part traditional patrol, resistance to the team by the non-team segment was almost automatic. In New York, where a 30-officer team was part of a 300-officer precinct, the team found it difficult to function cohesively since the officers remained part of the larger professional and social unit. In contrast, Holyoke's first team was geographically isolated from the rest of the force, having its own building and functioning both professionally and socially as a separate unit.

Selecting the Team Members

Most of the projects began solely with volunteers. The volunteering process produced primarily young officers with more than average enthusiasm and ambition. The decision to volunteer was often influenced by a variety of factors: peer group pressure, anticipated status, respect for the official who was soliciting volunteers, and the manner in which the volunteers were solicited. The volunteering seemed to have little connection to the substantive nature of the programs; most volunteers would have joined any new program.

In Syracuse, Lt. Sardino was asked by then Chief O'Connor to recruit team members. He talked with seven experienced officers who volunteered. The nature of the program at that point was vague, and the department's rank and file had not been involved in the planning. A year later, however, it was hard to attract good officers for the expanding program. By then, the rank and file had a fixed, if not necessarily accurate, conception of what team policing was all about, and most of them were against it. Sardino turned to new recruits; the department's training program became highly oriented to team methods and it successfully stimulated recruit enthusiasm.

In Los Angeles, officers for the original Basic Car Plan were selected in each patrol division by the division commander on the advice of the sergeants and lieutenants. The officers of Los Angeles' Team 28 in Venice were deliberately selected to test team policing as a technique with potential for broad application. Top-rated, middle-rated, and low-rated officers were assigned to the team in a ratio reflecting the entire department.

In Holyoke, 30 randomly selected officers were ordered to attend several weekend sessions conducted by outside consultants John Angell and Ray Galvin. At these sessions, a fairly intensive effort was made to explain to potential team members the general concept of team policing. To the surprise of the consultants, 25 officers volunteered when the sessions were concluded. Fourteen were selected.

Dayton followed the most complex and rigorous procedures, using both psychological testing and community screening. Eighty patrol officers of the 250-man force volunteered to undergo psychological testing. Thirty-nine police officers were selected and their names were circulated among various community groups in the 5th District. Community residents objected to the selection of two, and Chief Igleburger removed one from the program. Five of the patrol officers had been previously assigned as detectives. Their resignation from the high-status detective bureau underlined the initial success of the attempt to raise the status and self-image of patrol. The 39 patrolmen elected four sergeants and chose the sergeant they wanted to work under. Although the complex psychological and political selection proceedings employed in Dayton did not ultimately produce team members remarkably different from the rest of the force, it may have produced a sense of commitment to the concept of team policing.

Dayton's team members have by and large remained committed despite continuing resistance by the bulk of the force.

Only the teams in New York and Detroit considered race as a recruitment factor. In both cities, more than half of the team officers serving black neighborhoods were black themselves, in striking contrast to the rest of the predominantly white (90%) forces. The blacks on the teams usually lived in the city (though not necessarily in their team neighborhood), while the whites generally lived in the suburbs. Although the Los Angeles Department made an effort to assign Spanish-speaking officers to its teams, in none of the cities besides New York and Detroit did the racial composition of the team reflect a major departure from that of the rest of the force.

Should a team reflect the ethnic characteristics of its neighborhood? Sergeant Ambrose's team in New York City, half-white, half-black in an almost all black neighborhood, was accepted by the neighborhood to a degree that would seem unlikely if the team had been all white. Conversely, the Holyoke team achieved success in a heavily Puerto Rican neighborhood though none of its members were Puerto Rican. However, its Community Service Officers were Puerto Rican, and it was publicly announced that these CSO's were on a ladder to full-officer status. Furthermore, empathy in a more general sense was clearly helpful, and the Holyoke officers took an open and active interest in Puerto Rican culture, as seen by the signs in Spanish outside the team headquarters.

Training

The training of team police members was often not a formal process. In a majority of the programs, the team members had been left out of the planning; consequently, few were aware of the nature of the program and many had erroneous ideas about it. For example, in Detroit, where the program never emerged from the pilot stage, some police officers saw the project as an opportunity to "take the gloves off and really clean up this neighborhood." Because the word "team" suggested wide varieties of behavior, it became the job of the trainers to first explain the goals and then to translate them into "do's and don'ts."

Should team police officers be aggressive, stopping citizens to demand identification? Should they forsake preventive patrol and try foot patrol near their cars, talking to people in a friendly manner? Is a team member different from a regular patrol officer? If so, how? These are important questions, basic to the proper functioning of the team police officer on the street, which training programs could have addressed. The degree to which they were addressed influenced the degree to which team policing resulted in actual changes on the street and in the neighborhoods.

Available money and available manpower are basic considerations in planning training. Smaller departments often found it relatively easy to finance extensive training. In terms of training efficiency, however, a larger department had an advantage, since it could absorb the diversion of officers from patrol more easily and could train them as a unit. Dayton, on the other hand, had to divide its team-to-be in half for training, since all 40 officers could not be spared from the street at the same time.

The experience of seven cities indicates that the basic elements of team policing cannot be achieved without training. Whether the training is in the form of participation in planning, good on-the-job training, or formal classroom education, it is essential. Some changes in police departments can be made by fiat, but changes of the nature envisioned in team policing can be made only when the patrol officers understand and support them.

Experience also indicates that the process of training may be much more significant than the subjects taught. In Holyoke, as noted, the planning process was the training process. At a series of Saturday conferences, the consultants made it clear that the patrol officers were responsible for the planning. During the first months of the project, all of the Holyoke officers traveled in groups of two's and three's to at least one other city to view a team or related program, including Oakland, Los Angeles, Dayton, Minneapolis, and New York. The single formal component of the Holyoke training was a criminal investigation course at the local junior college.

The Holyoke training grew and changed from day to day. In contrast, Dayton's four-week training program was precisely planned in advance. The first two weeks focused on conflict management, the third on investigations. The fourth week was to have been used to sensitize the officers to the racially-mixed community by having officers live with local families for three to five days.[19] But this neatly structured program produced far less change in street policing styles than did Holyoke's more fluid process.

The most successful training involved field visits to other cities. For example, in New York the Planning Division, after choosing the first four target areas and sergeant team leaders, sent each sergeant to visit a team program in either Dayton, Detroit or Los Angeles. When they returned, they met with high-ranking officials to work out the details of New York's program. The result was a radical departure from tradition and a program that the sergeants felt proud to implement. Unfortunately, the later rapid expansion of the program prevented a similar training experience for each new team sergeant. The importance of the training was reflected in the difference between the first teams run by trained sergeants and the later teams run by untrained sergeants.

In the summer of 1972, the New York Training Division assigned two trainers to each of the five precincts which had become total team operations. The trainers worked with the team members and leaders, concentrating on three basic areas: team management, conflict control, and building community relations. The trainers adjusted the training to the needs of the officers and the realities of each neighborhood. In some precincts they met resistance from precinct commanders who wanted them to teach the officers how to fill out bureaucratic forms rapidly and accurately, but time and possibly support from the top resolved that difficulty.

Holyoke and Los Angeles' Team 28 particularly focused on molding a working team, while Dayton and Syracuse focused primarily on improving individuals' skills. In practice, the team approach seemed more successful. If the team is to function, make decisions and develop strategies as a team, then the process has to be learned from the beginning.

Dayton's efforts illustrate the problems created when insufficient attention is given to the team. Due to manpower shortages on the street, the entire group of 40 assigned to the Fifth District was split into two groups for the program. Each group functioned fairly well on its own, meeting daily at the academy. But when the two groups came together for their first and only full meeting, they floundered. They were able to make only one major decision and delegated further decisions to subcommittees which quickly fell apart.

---

[19]In fact, however, the department was unable to locate willing black families. The fourth training week was described *ex post facto* as "getting acquainted with the business and social organizations within the Fifth District."

The one major decision the group did make served to cripple it for further group action. By a virtually unanimous vote, the group decided to depart from the department's traditional policy of fixed tours of duty and adopt a schedule of three equal-sized shifts rotating on a weekly basis. Not only did this continue the worst feature of the old shift system (equal allocation of manpower for unequal periods of workload), but it also instituted new drawbacks: impaired health through fluctuating sleeping schedules and inconsistency of the police personnel interacting with the various street populations at different times of the day. One result of the fluctuating schedules was that officers who had originally agreed to come in on off-duty time for team meetings later refused.

What was omitted from the Dayton training was exactly the area in which the team failed—the dynamics of working together as a group. The Holyoke team learned group process by doing it during the planning stage. The Dayton program focused entirely on the way the individual, professional police officer related to his community (as investigator, crisis manager, and service provider). The result was a collection of individual police officers relating to the community but not to each other. It should be noted, however, that most training programs faced a choice of emphasis. Holyoke's training emphasized new organization concepts. Dayton taught behavioral concepts and skills and may have trained individual police officers better than Holyoke. The reaction of Dayton team officers to a crowd of black juveniles seemed relatively calm. The Holyoke officers, however, tended to become tense at the sight of a crowd, but could offer a conceptual explanation for what they were doing in terms of fairly sophisticated organizational theory. Dayton team officers, on the other hand, had a better knowledge than most other teams of the subtle psychological skills which police need (such as handling family disturbances). The Los Angeles Venice team, nevertheless, acquired both skills and organization concepts. The experience to date suggests that training, rather than being limited by a patrol officer's learning capacity, has only been limited by the imagination of the training designers. Emphasis need not have been a choice—both areas could have been taught.

Chapter IV
Team Policing on the Street

The most critical aspect of team policing is the complex process of moving from plan to fact, from lecture hall to street. It often begins at a well-attended press conference. Local community figures have their pictures taken drinking coffee with the team. After the party the team leader gives a pep talk, and the officers take to the streets. The press is likely to accept the goal as fact—a new, almost revolutionary type of "friendly" policing has been born. The assumption is that the team now belongs to the neighborhood, that it will, in a sense, take its shape in response to neighborhood conditions and that the neighborhood in turn will respond in a new and favorable way to police.

It was not long, however, before the team members noticed that their team policing hardly differed from the "policing" they had done before. In most cases, the style of police work changed very little under team policing. But it is impossible to say whether the organizational style of team policing failed to produce a new patrol style, or whether the organizational style of team policing was not, in those cases, created at all.

Stability of Assignment

The first thing team police officers in most of the cities noticed on the street was that they did not stay in their "neighborhood." With the exception of Dayton, Holyoke, and Venice, each team was dispatched close to half of its work time outside the boundaries of its neighborhood. Because 10,000-20,000 people lived within the neighborhood boundaries, it would have been hard enough for the team to develop area knowledge had they stayed in the area all the time. With only half their time spent in the neighborhood, area knowledge became an impossible goal.

The immediate effect of assignment out of the area was to make the patrol officer cynical about the entire team concept. If the first and most basic element of team policing was a hoax, why wasn't the rest? They all viewed the problem as the reason they could not get to know the community better: "We don't have time to stop and talk because we have to handle all those jobs outside the area."

Not all the fault lay with the dispatcher and the dispatching system, however. Many of the team patrol officers left their area on their own initiative. Bored with riding up and down their own streets, they left either to assist another car on a call or just to change the scenery. This side of the problem is not so much an organization failure as a training failure.

Team Relationship With the Community

Some teams became true neighborhood teams and established special, positive give-and-take relationships with their communities. Although most teams made some effort to do so, they sometimes confused "community" with "public" relations. Public relations was primarily an attempt to create a favorable image—certainly an improvement over previous relations, though not sufficient for the goals of team policing. It was most likely to occur when a team program was brand new. For example, a New York team commander visited most of the stores and businesses in his area and told his men to pay follow-up visits, an effort which reflected a salesman-like frame of mind: "Try to sell the storeowner that he's getting more police protection (even though we know he's not)." Letters of commendation were often solicited; in fact, one businessman distributed to other businessmen mimeographed letters addressed to the police commissioner, commending the team. There was a space for signatures at the bottom. In Los Angeles, the police practiced public relations on a continuing basis with the original Basic Car Plan. Each car team held a monthly community meeting at a neighborhood school. The goal was commendable, but the meetings failed to encourage dialogue since they relied on pre-packaged programs. Later, Los Angeles' Team 28 in Venice built more wisely. With its system of block captains, home protection visits and "coffee klatches," it engaged the citizens in give-and-take sessions, out of which grew a continuing, knowledgeable, and productive community of shared purpose.

Some teams realized that public and private welfare and medical organizations were also potential tools for building community acceptance. In New York, NPT police officers were told to refer addicts to rehabilitation centers, but many officers continued to ignore or arrest the addicts. The Dayton team did make arrangements with health agencies for 24-hour reception of alcoholics, and other agencies agreed to help the police handle juveniles in trouble and married couples in conflict. The Dayton team did not use these resources extensively, but they did use them more than any other teams observed.

Teams needed to be accepted by most citizens in a neighborhood, but they needed more than acceptance—they needed active support. The Venice team developed direct citizen support to an extraordinary degree. Hundreds of block captains exchanged crime information with police on a regular basis. The Holyoke team caught more than one burglar after citizen calls traced them out of windows, down alleys, over fences, and across the railroad tracks. The team in The Flats virtually abandoned preventive patrol since the citizenry informed them immediately of many crimes in progress. Such citizen support was essential, since crimes are solved because citizens cooperate; even if most crimes could be solved by detective story deduction (and they cannot), the cost would be prohibitive. In small cities, or in closely knit neighborhoods in larger cities, information passes swiftly from neighbor to neighbor. If the people accept the police as part of the community, they share the information with them. The first Crime Control Team in Syracuse was in a stable, all white, lower-middle-class area in which many policemen resided or had been raised. An intensive police campaign was launched to encourage citizens to report anything suspicious. As in Holyoke, police soon found they could trace fleeing burglars by means of citizen phone calls. Unfortunately, community support in black and hippie neighborhoods was not so easily developed. The police were reluctant to establish relationships, and the citizens had a strong ethic against "ratting" or "finking." Most New York City teams failed to develop anything approximating a community network, but as noted, Sergeant Robert Crowley of the 6th

Precinct Neighborhood Police Team in New York's Greenwich Village was able to gather information by attending group meetings and talking about crime problems with the articulate, upper-middle-class residents. These residents had not thought of calling the police with incidental intelligence, but they were enthusiastic when Crowley came to them.

Dayton and Holyoke organized their team programs to include policy-making by the community. Both have community boards composed of representatives chosen by local groups—Parent-Teacher Associations, civic associations, block clubs, tenant organizations, etc. And both have listened to their boards and followed their advice. In Dayton, the community advisors rejected two officers recommended for the teams (although only one was ultimately rejected by the department), pointed out performance deficiencies, and went to City Hall to lobby for funds for team policing. The Holyoke board has been tied closely to the Model Cities Board in The Flats. Their initial concern had been the cultural clashes between French and Puerto Ricans. Before the team became operational, much community conflict had been generated by police attempts to enforce the laws against public drinking. The Puerto Rican community had been reluctant to abandon its front-stoop beer drinking to satisfy American middle-class notions of propriety, and there had been a number of assaults on policemen and one shooting. The team ignored the stoop drinking, and for a year there were no assaults on police officers and no citizen complaints.

Citizens on Patrol

As late as the early 19th century, the "hue and cry" was the most common urban means of catching criminals. From the time of ancient Athens—where all eighteen-year-old males were conscripted for two years' duty in "preserving the public order"—until the Industrial Revolution, the citizens had the responsibility for keeping the peace and catching criminals. The Industrial Revolution increased the size and density of cities, created new problems of public order, and made professional police departments a necessity. "Hue and cry" passed into oblivion. So, to a degree, did the dangers of vigilantism and mob justice. Unfortunately, the pendulum continues to swing. During the last decade, acts of vandalism and even rapes and murders have begun and been completed in full view of passersby. A recent incident in New York's Times Square area produced a reverse "hue and cry"—a menacing crowd intervened after a bank holdup to prevent the bank guard from apprehending the holdup suspect.

Despite professional reservations, police in Dayton, New York, and Los Angeles have all officially encouraged citizen patrol. Dayton's citizen program is directly related to the team. The concept is not new; the British have a highly developed system, and New York and Boston have had active auxiliary forces since the World War II civil defense warden program. New York, which now has 3,000, once had 20,000. The New York volunteers wear a uniform similar to the regulars, although their silver star badge resembles a child's toy. They carry nightsticks but not guns. Their arrest powers are no more than those of ordinary citizens. Reporting through their own command structure, they rarely work with regular police officers, although they are now allowed to ride along in police cars and one precinct even allows the auxiliary patrol to use police cars on their own. A large number of the volunteers are black and Puerto Rican (a much larger proportion than on the regular force).

Dayton made an effort to select its Neighborhood Assistance Officers with care and to limit their activities. They were intended to relieve the regular teams of paperwork and a range of traffic and service functions. A limit of 50 active male and female NAO's was set by a board of directors composed of representatives of all interested community organizations. LEAA funding paid for: (1) an 80-hour training program at the police academy, (2) a director and assistant director to be employed on a part-time basis, to do applicant screening, performance evaluation, and administrative record keeping, and (3) the purchase of walkie-talkies for contacting central dispatch. The NAO's worked at least 20 hours a month; a typical tour of duty was performed by two citizens in a private car from 6:00 p.m. to 10:00 or midnight. The bulk of the time was spent driving up and down the Fifth District's pretty tree-lined streets of comfortable and neatly kept homes, looking for burglars and people who "look like they don't belong here." While the NAO's did provide genuine assistance to the police, the Dayton experience pointed up the danger that citizen patrols could contribute to stronger anti-police attitudes in parts of the community.

Since team policing desires to make the police a more personal part of the community, it seems sensible to attempt to bring independent community patrols under the team wing. When an adversarial, predominantly black, adult community patrol group developed in Brooklyn's 77th Precinct, Neighborhood Police Team commander Sgt. William Ambrose persuaded them to join his team. As a major incentive, he was able to obtain walkie-talkies for his foot-patrolling volunteers, so that any street crime witnessed could be reported immediately. Team commander Anthony Quatrone, in the nearby 71st Precinct, a transition area of blacks and elderly whites, was faced with three successive elevator murders of elderly white people. When a supplemental community patrol began to form, Quatrone channeled the energy into tenant patrols inside buildings. In addition to scheduling periodic checks on each floor, these patrols also stimulated the very neighborly (as well as crime-preventive) practice of evening card games and knitting groups in the apartment lobbies. While not part of the Neighborhood Police Team, the tenant groups were frequently visited and encouraged by Quatrone and his men.

Team Members as Investigators

The authority to handle investigations was for many team members the most significant part of team policing. Detectives, who traditionally conducted all follow-up investigations, were viewed as an elite group who got the "hot" cases. The team policy, giving considerable follow-up investigation responsibility to team members, was accepted as a challenge. The scope of investigative responsibilities varied from city to city. The Holyoke and Dayton teams handled their own investigations with good results. Holyoke had an advantage—readily available overtime pay which permitted an officer to continue a "hot" investigation beyond his normal tour of duty. In one case an officer on the 4:00 p.m. to midnight shift received a complaint of an auto theft at 10:00 p.m. By interrogating bystanders he obtained a description of the man who had driven the car away. As he was writing his report about 2:00 a.m., a concerned citizen came in with two tires that he had just purchased from a stranger; his brother had suggested that the tires were stolen and warned him that he would be liable to arrest. The description of the tireseller matched that of the auto thief. By 10:00 a.m., the officer had apprehended the suspect and recovered the stolen auto.

Dayton intended to make overtime pay available to its team police officers, but the municipal budget crisis ended that plan. When an officer conducting an investigation finished a tour of duty, the investigation was delayed until his next tour. Important cases were sometimes turned over to a team officer coming on duty, but the natural competition for making good arrests discouraged frequent use of this approach. Even so, the Dayton team was heavily involved in investigations, handling all crimes except homicide. Each officer carried many cases, sometimes for weeks. Having the authority to close or file cases, they tended to concentrate on the most recent, filing away the older ones.

However, the Dayton teams did not conduct case conferences. Consequently, information collected by each team patrol officer was not always shared with the others, although bulletin board notices of major situations helped to fill this gap. If information had been properly collected and collated, however, patterns of crime could have been discerned. The weekly rotation of shifts (12-8, 8-4, 4-12) provided an opportunity—sooner or later—to question people who were available only at specific times, but the shifts made it harder for community people to contact individual officers.

In Syracuse and New York, outside investigative specialists still invaded the team's territory for special problems or assignments. The Syracuse Crime Control Team began with a working rule that if a case developed no leads within an hour's work, it should be closed. The focus was on crime control, not solution—"concern for the future and not for the past." Time spent on investigations was considered time lost from preventive patrol; attempts to apprehend suspects after the fact hindered attempts to apprehend perpetrators during the act. When Dr. Elliott, the project director, later sought to put a greater emphasis on investigations, the team's patterns had already been set. The officers, therefore, rarely attempted much follow-up on any of their cases, although their immediate efforts produced a respectable clearance rate.

In New York City, patrol officers throughout the department had been given responsibility for preliminary investigations. No changes in the handling of follow-up investigations, however, were made for team officers. Some felt this was because New York traditionally maintained a sharp distinction between patrol officers and detectives. Patrol officers resented the stereotype of an arrogant detective who arrived at the scene and immediately dismissed them, but they accepted it as an inevitable part of the system. Detectives were ultimately assigned to the teams, rather than increasing the investigative responsibility of the team patrol officers.

Team Leadership: The Role of the Sergeant

Leadership, more than any other factor, determined the way team officers worked on the street. Team leaders who used new, innovative styles of leadership had dramatic effects on the performance of their teams. The leadership of the lieutenants and sergeants in the Venice District of Los Angeles, for instance, was clearly a new style, as was the leadership of some sergeants in New York. Many team leaders, however, continued the same old style of supervision they had used before team policing, and their patrol officers often continued the old style of police work.

Most police administrators who implemented team policing were aware of the traditional view which first-line supervisors (sergeants) have taken of their job, even in "professionalized" departments: (1) exercise only as much control over patrolmen as the higher-ups demand, and (2) do as little work as possible. Those police administrators sought to make leaders out of sergeants who had always been supervisors. Their concept of team policing was that sergeants should use less control (discipline, orders, and "checking up") and more support (planning, training, information exchange) in dealing with their patrol officers. Unfortunately, team sergeants rarely practiced that concept.

Several team leaders understood their role to require both increased support and control, but most only understood that they were to decrease their control. This decreased control was criticized by opponents of team policing. Nonetheless, the real problem of team policing—often simply a failure to do anything new or different—was due more to the lack of support from team leaders than to a lack of control. But the fact that most police departments found it difficult to develop a new leadership style for team policing should not be cause for pessimism. One should be more impressed by the fact that in more than half the departments, leaders did emerge and did develop decentralized professional styles of police work.

The first-level team leader was usually relatively young, with approximately ten years on the force. Except for some New York City team leaders, all were white. Most had military service, and all were selected for "above-average leadership ability." In both Syracuse and Dayton, the sergeant team commanders led 10-member teams. They reported to a lieutenant who was in charge of all teams. The team sergeants and the lieutenant shared supervisory responsibility for all 40 to 50 team officers, with no help from other superiors. In New York, one sergeant alone commanded 40 to 50 officers in one neighborhood police team. In his absence, however, any other precinct sergeant could step in and issue orders. In Holyoke, the "democratic colleague" team was chaired by an elected patrol officer and coordinated by a captain; there were no other ranks in the team, and no outside officers commanded the men.

Old vs. New Supervision

The Syracuse Police Department, following the reform administrations of the mid-1960's, had been strongly oriented to hierarchical structure, stern discipline, and strict adherence to rules and procedures. Sergeants had ensured that no patrolman smoked or removed his hat while on duty. Dr. J. F. Elliott, the physicist from General Electric, saw this atmosphere of tight control as counterproductive to both the control of crime and the professionalization of the police. Arguing that a fundamental characteristic of professionalism is freedom to exercise discretion, Elliott persuaded Chief O'Connor to incorporate patrol officer self-direction into the Crime Control Team. For the team leaders this change created a new role of coordinator, analyzer of crime patterns, collector and distributor of information, trainer, and major liaison to the community. In order to insure that the new role would be performed capably, a lieutenant was designated to lead the first Crime Control Team. Subsequent teams, however, were led by sergeants, all of whom were coordinated by a lieutenant.

With new roles for both patrol officers and first-line supervisors, the team members were free of many old restraints—they did not have to attend roll calls, they could follow up cases on their own, and except for the 40 hours each week that the team leaders were on duty, they were free of direct supervision. This meant, as it worked out, that they were particularly free of supervision on Saturday night, since the sergeants chose never to work on weekends. One sergeant who later left the CCT said to an observer, "Those kids were crying for help; you can't make generals out of privates." And, indeed, to the extent that the team leaders failed to provide the support functions of coordination, crime analysis, information exchange, and training, the patrol officers did suffer from a lack of direction. The old style of heavy supervision had been abandoned, but it had not been replaced by any new supportive leadership with a firm, if light, touch. The sergeants found it very difficult to see themselves as generators of ideas or enthusiasm. The actual amount of supervisory presence at police-handled field situations was probably no less than it was before—supervisors had rarely been present anyway—but the formalization of the patrol officer's freedom ran counter to tradition, and non-team sergeants and lieutenants frequently came into CCT neighborhoods and gave orders as if to maintain the myth of close supervision.

In Venice, the team functioned in its daily decisions as a separate police department. The sergeants were leaders and coordinators, responsible for planning strategies; the lieutenant was a mini-police chief. In practice, a high degree of coordination and participatory management was achieved by skillful leadership and much communication.

Under the Basic Car Plan, the Los Angeles police, traditionally a spit-and-polish, militaristic and highly "professional" organization in the technical sense, had a form of supervision under which a sergeant commanded a consistent group of men in a given geographic area, who all worked on the same watch. He rarely intervened, more often discussing and criticizing the patrol officer's performance after the situation was over. The sergeant did not attend as many situations as he might have, however.

Team policing requires a personal and consistent relationship between the team leader, usually a sergeant, and the team members. Both New York and Detroit have traditionally lacked consistent relationships between one sergeant and a group of patrol officers. In both cities, officers have been assigned to beats and sergeants to entire precincts. The patrol officer never felt that it was "his" sergeant who evaluated his performance.

In New York, the structural remoteness was reinforced by a scarcity of sergeants, with a ratio of 25 officers to one sergeant instead of the common ratio of 10 to 1. Although Detroit's ratio was about 10 to 1, the effective ratio was cut in half by the traditional practice of two sergeants riding in the same car; one sergeant riding with a patrol officer (as in New York) or alone (as in Los Angeles) makes more sergeants available for more incidents.

In setting up teams first in Detroit and then in New York, Commissioner Murphy sought to establish a consistent relationship between a sergeant and a particular group of patrol officers, thus changing the sergeant from a distant, apathetic, occassionally authoritarian monitor into a personal leader responsible for all police work and crime conditions within his area. This responsible role meant that the sergeant would become an "analyst, planner, director, information systems developer, leader, as well as community relations specialist; hopefully, he will become a highly respected community leader." In order to perform these functions effectively, the team commanders were given maximum flexibility in the deployment and utilization of their men. They were not, however, given control over non-patrol activities of the police within their areas.

The building of mutual reliance between patrol officers and sergeants had some dangers. In New York, where there was great pressure from above to perform, the only alliance of sergeant and patrol officer traditionally was a conspiracy to beat the system; sergeants would tell the patrol officers, "Don't you bother me and I won't bother you to pick up the phone (answer the radio)." This may be a problem peculiar to large, crime-burdened traditional departments. In Holyoke, Los Angeles, and Richmond, the close alignment of sergeants and team patrol officers worked to promote productivity.

It must be emphasized that team leaders are not simply supervisors whose job it is to see that no one "goofs-off." They have more challenging duties. In Dayton, they (and the lieutenant) theoretically spent most of their time giving individual attention to special community problems, many outside of the traditional law enforcement role—e.g., giving advice in landlord-tenant disputes and securing services from other municipal agencies. The captain in Holyoke performed a similar role. Both cities stressed the concept that the patrol officers had individual responsibility for providing police service to the community; the absence of supervisors checking up on them dramatically illustrated the faith and the trust the department and the community had in the patrol officer. In theory, the existence of a system of control challenged the patrol officer to try to beat it; the absence assumed he would be motivated by his own sense of duty. Holyoke's and Venice's democratic team models facilitated the leader's role as an advisor with veto power rather than as a roll call autocrat.[20]

---

[20]As the Holyoke team became more controversial, the team members apparently felt vulnerable. The captain's response was to tell them they really wanted more direction and they agreed. Nevertheless, the evidence seems to show that the democratic method of operation continued and the team members participated as before.

Team leaders often faced the competing demands of office work and field work. For example, many of the projects required detailed narrative and statistical reports each month. And, if teams were to manage themselves and plan their own strategies and tactics, they needed data support. Analysis of crime patterns, evaluation of patrol activity reports, information exchanges with other municipal agencies serving the community, and planning papers for future community needs were all important. In Venice, Team 28 had the full-time service of a civilian administrative aide who did much of this work, but the team leaders still felt that the development of a separate administrative group to support the field work would be useful.

Communications Within the Team

The ideal police team leader would have developed a group of officers whose activities were fully complemented, based on policy decisions arrived at from a complete exchange of information on current area conditions. The major responsibility of the team leader could be viewed as facilitating the coordination, information exchange, and policy-making functions of the team. While most team leaders were fully aware of the importance of this responsibility, they often lacked the tools and skills with which to carry it out.

A frequently tried (and abandoned) tool was the team conference. In the 77th Precinct's Neighborhood Police Team in New York, Sgt. William Ambrose and his team met each Monday at 3:30 p.m. (officers on the 8:00 a.m. to 4:00 p.m. watch returned early and those on the 4:00 p.m. to 12 midnight came in early). At one such session, Sgt. Ambrose evaluated the performances of the patrol officers in enforcing the Sanitary Code, made routine announcements, and then opened the meeting to discussion. One officer mentioned purse-snatching near the welfare center on "Mother's Day," the semi-monthly distribution date for welfare checks, and another suggested a tactic: put an officer on a roof overlooking the block with a walkie-talkie, and another on the street in plain clothes. When the first spotted a mugger he would alert the officer on the ground. The suggested tactic was discussed and accepted. A black patrolman reminded the whites of the community anger over recent welfare reductions. Sgt. Ambrose told the team to be tough on double parking because of the fire hazard when cars block narrow streets.

Ambrose's meetings were successful but not fully attended; no feasible way was found to bring in officers from the midnight to 8:00 a.m. shift. Since Ambrose scheduled his officers on the basis of workload and since few worked midnight to 8:00, their absence was not critical; but full coordination was difficult without full attendance. Many New York police officers lived over an hour's traveling time from their jobs, and it was impractical for them to come to brief meetings during their off-hours. In Los Angeles and Holyoke, where overtime money was available, schedules were adjusted so that the entire team occasionally worked a full shift together, and the shift included the conference.

There were other, more subtle, problems in conference planning. In low-crime cities, there was often little to talk about, and frequent conferences became a bore. In Dayton the team members wasted time complaining about faulty equipment, uncooperative courts, and other elements beyond their control. In some cities, team leaders lacking experience in leading group discussions found it difficult to keep the group focused on productive discussion. In other cases, strong leaders dominated the proceedings to a point where the conferences became merely lectures. Many team leaders found the whole process too difficult and simply abandoned it.

The formal conference, however, is not the only possible tool available to the leaders for coordination, information exchange, and policy making. Roll calls, change of personnel in patrol cars, and mealtimes provided informal occasions for coordination. The Venice team in Los Angeles furnished officers with daily computer print-outs of crimes and the civilian block captains with weekly ones. When a team was sufficiently small, as in Dayton and Holyoke, coordination could be accomplished informally. The 14-member Holyoke team rarely had more than three or four officers on duty, and they were constantly in touch with each other. The same was true of the subteams in Dayton, where the entire manpower for each beat was two officers in one car; since the area contained four beats, six to eight officers were doing field work at any given time. In Richmond three or four team members often responded together to a single call.

The greater problem of coordination was between officers working different shifts. Particularly in teams that work steady tours of duty (e.g., an officer is assigned consistently to the 8-4 tour for a month or more), there is a natural tendency to form a team around those officers who are on duty together. Rather than having a small geographical area team, a larger geographic area time team develops. Even the small English teams have experienced this problem:

> The panda car crew is part of a team comprised of the men themselves, the two area constables, the detective assigned to the car beat and in most instances a sergeant who has special responsibility for that car beat. Many of the panda car drivers we spoke to felt that their greatest loyalty was with the shift of men with whom they worked regularly as opposed to the officers we envisaged would form the team. The development of team spirit amongst officers working on a particular car beat is proving rather difficult while there is ample evidence of a keen team spirit amongst officers working together on the same tour of duty.[21]

Since face-to-face association produced team spirit and coordination, the simplest way to foster them was to increase the amount of face-to-face contact between officers on different shifts. A team leader sometimes built an informal communication network by suggesting the members exchange home telephone numbers and socialize after hours.

Team Flexibility: Schedules, Uniforms

Team leaders had wide discretion each day for the scheduling of officers, but in fact they often used the easiest method—assigning an equal number of officers to each shift despite clear evidence that service calls and reported crimes varied widely hour-to-hour and day-to-day. Holyoke established working schedules purely on the basis of workload (though Holyoke had a relatively light workload at any time). Richmond built its whole team effort on the principle of flooding the streets with officers during high-crime periods and almost emptying them during low-crime times. In New York, the team leader theoretically had complete control over scheduling, but the precinct clerical patrol officer who formerly ran the precinct (as the captain's "executive vice president") was often reluctant to yield his authority. As the teams in New York grew larger—from 30 to 50 officers—the team leader was often happy to have the "clerical man" do the scheduling. Many team sergeants did put most of their officers on the heavy-duty shifts between 8:00 a.m. and midnight, but few attempted to analyze workload patterns more thoroughly or to examine, for example, the possible efficiency of overlapping shifts or beginning shifts at unorthodox times.

---

[21]Home Office Report on Unit Beat Policing, 1967.

Team leaders and teams often failed to explore other possibilities as well—such as innovations and varieties of dress. In Dayton, Chief Robert M. Igleburger encouraged the teams to dress as they wished, saying, "You've been trying to get out of the 'bag' for years, anyway." The team, strongly influenced by the first team leader, decided to wear the traditional police uniform most of the time. Although some chose to wear ordinary plain clothes on occasion, they declined to wear slacks and blazers in the fashion of Holyoke.

The uniform issue in New York was a bit more complex. The idea of disguises was already fully accepted—police disguised as taxi and truck drivers had caught hold-up persons, and plainclothes men and women had intercepted muggers and served as decoys to catch rapists. The teams found these tactics worthwhile, but the use of ordinary plain clothes proved more difficult. Police in plain clothes had been used traditionally in fields particularly susceptible to corruption—gambling, prostitution, and narcotics. A team sergeant in Harlem attempted to put plainclothes officers on patrol behind apartment buildings to reduce daytime residential burglaries, but his captain, worried about the possibility of inviting corruption (or the suspicion of corruption), vetoed the idea. A subsequent survey by the Urban Institute showed that virtually none of the NPT commanders were using such plainclothes tactics—probably because of the anti-crime plainclothes programs that were being conducted by precinct commanders at the same time.

Summary

Many of the plans for team policing failed to materialize, and the most direct cause of that failure was the performance of team leaders. However, their performance was shaped by the larger organizational context. Given the problems of middle management (the leaders' bosses), the usual trial by peers, and dispatching policy—all to be discussed in the next chapter—it is not surprising that the team leaders failed to create the team style as planned.

Chapter V
Obstacles to
Team Policing

In addition to the inevitable influence of individual leaders, police department organization contributed three major obstacles to team policing: middle management, trial by peers, and dispatchers.

Middle Management

Team policing, as a method of decentralization, was designed to give more decision-making power to lower levels of the police organization. By fiat from the top, it gave powers to the bottom (patrol officers and sergeants) that had traditionally been reserved for the middle (lieutenants, captains, etc.). Thus team policing was a form of decentralization which gave less power to mid-management than it had under centralization. As a result, middle management often impeded their administrators' goals for team policing.

One way in which middle management limited the success of team policing was by failing, as precinct or division commanders, to deal with conflicts and problems arising out of team policing programs under their command. Conflicts frequently developed between team leaders and officers of the next higher rank—a problem apparently endemic to the team policing concept. It surfaced in England almost immediately, where despite the role definitions of inspectors as strategists and sergeants as tacticians, one Home Office study found that both ranks were confused and dissatisfied about their new roles. Detroit and

New York had similar conflicts between lieutenants and sergeants that the precinct commanders simply ignored.

Another, more direct way in which middle management sometimes thwarted the goals of team policing was by simple bad-mouthing: sending out the word through informal channels of communication that this crazy team idea was a hoax. Precinct commanders were also able to undercut the operational freedom of the team leader. By limiting or discouraging the team leader's initiative on day-to-day issues, middle management could effectively defeat the program's goal of innovative team response to local conditions.

A third form of resistance by middle management was a frank expression to top management of disagreement about team policing issues. A Detroit precinct commander complained to the police commissioner that by implication the Beat Commander system criticized the precinct commander's performance, implying that his position was insufficient to insure adequate police service. In his frustration he exclaimed, "The people who wrote the guidelines for this thing didn't read the rules and regulations." The view that the rules and regulations are sacred and unchangeable subverts not only team policing, but any change at all.

Middle-management opposition is not unavoidable, however. If middle management is brought into the planning process for decentralization, it is entirely possible that its cooperation and support for the new system will be won. Although the commander of the first precinct in a city to try the team concept was usually involved in its planning (Detroit, New York, Los Angeles), most of the middle managers who would be affected by the program were not asked for their views, nor were they told about the program before its public announcement. But a participative and consensual form of planning with all middle management can cultivate their support for plans which might otherwise be resisted.

Most team programs have been perceived as giving more power to the bottom at the expense of the middle, a perception which has been the basis for middle management's opposition. It is possible, however, for the power of each level to be expanded simultaneously with benefits for the entire organization. A goal of team policing is to expand the effectiveness of the police in the community: talking to more people, establishing more positive and informational relationships, apprehending more criminals, and providing more and better service.

This expanded role requires a new structure: the followers (patrol officers and sergeants) must do more leading of themselves, and the leaders (middle management) must lead in new and different ways. Mid-managers must analyze the new influx of information, plan for better manpower utilization in light of that information, and obtain more resources to support the expanded role of their officers—for example, arranging liaison with social service agencies, traffic and sanitation departments, and other city agencies. If their function is viewed more as support than as control, middle management can gain power under team policing rather than lose it.

Trial by Peers

Middle management was not the only obstacle to team policing. In most of the cities studied, the larger patrol force—those not involved in the team project—objected to team policing. The opposition was strongest when the project split a precinct or a division. The first pilot teams formed new elites. The patrol officers had learned to accept the old elite forces (e.g., detectives), but they were not eager to accept new ones. The fact that the usefulness of the teams was necessarily unproven left them vulnerable to attack. Also, to outside patrol officers, the community aspects of team policing smacked of appeasement of hostile minorities.

There was also jealousy, in many instances stemming from the fact that the patrol officers first heard about the program through the news media—after the personnel had already been chosen. Not all patrol officers would have volunteered, but many would have liked to have had the chance to decide not to. When one is shut out of a newly-formed club, the natural response is to attack the club—and certain aspects of team programs were "clubby" and, superficially at least, elitist. The first Crime Control Teams in Syracuse wore white shirts while the rest of the patrol force wore blue, which prompted sarcastic remarks such as "the good guys wear white shirts." In New York, the Neighborhood Police Team in the 17th Precinct (midtown) was exempted from consulate guard duty, a detested detail. The apparent over-allocation of manpower to NPT areas (even though justified by workload figures) produced the charge from other precinct patrol officers that they had all the hard work. Detroit's Beat Command invited resentment by flaunting their accomplishment of reducing the average time required to complete radio runs from 40 minutes to 27. The freedom of team police officers in some cities produced irritation. In Syracuse, for example, the CCT was freed from roll calls. In New York, the orders establishing the Neighborhood Police Teams suspended portions of the Rules and Procedures manual—one that had been frequently violated in the field, anyway—to legitimize such things as chatting with neighborhood people and driving sick cases to the hospital. The overtime pay available to the Holyoke team was greatly resented by other patrol officers of the poorly paid department.

Given all of these irritations, one might expect the outside patrol officers' field cooperation to be affected. With the exception of Holyoke (where the team had virtually seceded from the rest of the department), this did not happen. The team members were always backed up by non-team cars. None of the physical acts that too often characterize racial or religious animosity in police departments (vandalizing lockers, insulting graffiti, and even fights) occurred between team officers and the regular patrols. Instead, the opposition was evidenced by strong vocal criticism and political maneuvers to keep the team idea from spreading.

Dispatchers

Another non-team group, the radio dispatchers, greatly hampered team policing, often without intent. The dispatcher is under constant pressure, and he is not particularly concerned with neighborhood or team boundaries. He must be converted to the primary assumption that the new neighborhood team should stay in its neighborhood. Teams frequently could not; New York teams often spent half their time outside their neighborhoods. When the team members found the neighborhood was a myth, many concluded that the team project was a hoax.

Sociologist Albert Reiss has made an observation on the Chicago Police Department's dispatching system, which should be applicable to other large cities:

> In Chicago in 1966, we observe that fewer than one-third of all criminal incidents were handled by beat cars in their own beat . . . . Many police administrators regard a patrolman's intelligence on a community to be of most importance in non-criminal matters, where an officer must exercise the greatest degree of discretion. However, despite this, officers in Chicago handled an even smaller proportion of all non-criminal incidents, arising from dispatches to their own beat, than criminal incidents . . . . Beat cars handled only one-third of all incidents, and one-fifth of all criminal incidents arising on their own beats.

Based on these Chicago data, it appears conclusive that beat cars, whether dispatched or on routine preventive patrol, are more likely to handle incidents outside their own area than within it . . . . This problem may actually be due to the fact that beat cars are dispatched to handle incidents outside their beat. Once a car is dispatched to handle a call outside its beat, the probability of its handling outside calls increases, since, while that car is in service, any call to its beat must be assigned to a car from a neighboring beat. Calls to that beat in turn must be handled by a neighboring car. The problem of such chain effects is a familiar one in systems analysis.[22]

Today's radio systems give little latitude for the kind of screening which once occurred when calls came in at the precinct switchboard and the sergeant held the less important calls or threw out the ones from known neighborhood cranks. Computerized dispatch systems such as New York's SPRINT treat almost all calls as serious, and the widespread use of the "911" police telephone number has increased the volume enormously.

The Los Angeles Basic Car Plan attempted to cope with the dispatching problem. The "A" Basic Cars worked with "X" support cars on the heavy duty, 8:00 a.m. to 4:00 p.m. and 4:00 p.m. to midnight watches. The Basic Cars were to remain in their beats, while the X cars crossed boundaries. In practice, the distinction between A and X was often without substance. Dispatchers frequently assigned either, without regard for beats.

In Detroit, the Beat Command cars were out of their neighborhoods as much as a third of the time. Only after great pressure was placed on the dispatchers from the top did the percentage drop to 10-15%. The Detroit dispatchers were bitter about the pressure. They said the Beat Command car was often the closest car to the call, but they were forbidden to send it. In the end, the Detroit dispatchers gave the Beat Command cars no outside calls of any nature. They treated the two-sector area as an entirely separate precinct and sent cars from miles away to an emergency scene immediately adjoining the Beat Command boundaries even when the BC car was available. Obviously, city-wide application of this principle would be disastrous, turning the city into hundreds of non-cooperating police departments.

But the dispatchers are not the villains. Consider a huge roomful of clacking printers and blaring loudspeakers on a hot summer night

---

[22]Albert Reiss, *The Police and the Public* (New Haven: Yale University Press, 1971), pp. 98-99.

with calls backlogged for two hours. Each dispatcher has 30 to 70 sector cars to dispatch. If an available car happens to be labelled team, he will assign that car to the necessary job regardless. Indeed, the pressure grows so intense that in one city on an especially busy evening, a captain tried to prod a dispatcher into faster clearing of calls; the dispatcher, in response, stood up, vomited, threw his shield to the floor, gave his captain an obscene gesture, announced that he was reporting sick, and walked away.

There were reasons why team cars were often the most frequently available. The size of a team may be determined by a computation of precinct manpower to area workload. The logic of the method, however, had only one weakness: it was never used for the other sectors of the precinct. The result of making workload calculations for one area but not the others could result (and did) in the assignment of more officers to the team area and a decrease in the number in other areas. It was difficult to persuade others that team policing would make better use of available manpower when the apparent result was to double the manpower assigned to the team area while reducing it everywhere else. The second reason that the team cars in Detroit and New York were frequently available was that the number of team men on duty was (sometimes) related to time workload while the number of non-team men on duty was not. Teams which assigned the most officers during peak hours were unrushed while the rest of the precinct was backlogged with calls. Non-team officers concluded erroneously that the teams were not doing their share of the work.

The dispatching difficulty is not insurmountable, and it is not universal. There is relatively little boundary difficulty in Holyoke or in Venice (LA). In the dispatching issue, small cities or self-contained units like Venice have a clear advantage—the pressure is less and the boundaries are easier to maintain.

Chapter VI
Evaluations

T eam policing is a means to an end: a new organizational concept designed to produce a better kind of policing. An evaluation of the success of that concept in producing the desired end can be done only if the concept itself is fully put into practice. But in most of the seven cities studied, the team policing concept was never fully developed and put into practice. Consequently, most of this book has been about what happened in the course of trying to create team policing, rather than about the effects of those attempts on the quality of police service. Of the cities which had evaluations, few of them included both of these issues.

Research vs. Action

The state of the art in evaluation of social experiments is still very primitive, especially in police experiments.[23] Team policing confronted evaluators not only with problems of measuring such elusive data as the amount of real crime, but also with problems of conflict between research goals and action goals. Team policing, like many other institutional change efforts of the 1960's, was usually conducted as a demonstration project: one that demonstrates, on a limited scale, the presumed superiority of a new approach, prior to its adoption on a

---

[23]See Joseph H. Lewis, *Evaluation of Experiments in Policing: Where Do You Begin?* (Washington, D. C.: Police Foundation, 1972).

wider scale. In many instances, objectives were not clearly specified at the beginnings and evaluation considerations played little or no part in design of the demonstrations. When evaluation is "tacked on" at the end, it can rarely prove either what happened or what may have caused what is thought to have happened.

Many evaluators of demonstration projects have soundly taken the position that unless it is known precisely what a project has demonstrated (i.e., has it really reduced crime or improved response time), then there is no assurance that the innovation is an improvement.

Municipal agencies, however, usually take the view, and the public generally agrees, that they are mainly in business to deliver services and not to conduct research. The administrators, not the researchers, are in charge. They are legally and ethically bound to deliver the "best" service possible, regardless of research needs. It can be argued that the only way to provide "best" services in a changing world is to allocate some resources on a regular basis to research, as all successful industries do, to try things out and, if they do not work as well as hoped for or conditions change, to try other methods or tactics and compare the results.

This research/action dilemma cannot be solved in principle, only in practice. A police chief, committed to getting reliable data on how a project is working, and a researcher, sensitive to the political, operational and (even) psychological needs of a police department, can together produce both research and action.

Methods and Measurements

Every team experiment studied for this book had improved crime control as one of its goals. Yet none of them included an evaluation component which could measure the amount of real crime in the team areas. Reported crime records have long been recognized to be gross undercounts of real crime. Increased citizen confidence in the police, another goal of team policing, could lead to more crimes being reported even though real crime may be decreasing. The only available means for measuring real crime are victimization surveys, and they are extremely expensive. Yet, as Lewis notes, without research of this kind, team policing experiments are not worth doing as crime-control experiments. Other team policing goals were better measured in some of the cities that evaluated their teams.[24] But generally the evaluations were plagued by poorly specified objectives; poorly chosen (or no)

100

control or comparison groups or areas; failure to gather baseline, or "before," data; poorly designed data collection questionnaires; and weak quality control over interviewers. A crime-control evaluation industry has only begun to emerge in the last two or three years as some of the 1968 Safe Streets Act money has been invested in it, and like any new industry, its products have many bugs.

The Police Foundation has invested over two million dollars in a team policing experiment being conducted by the Cincinnati Police Division. The program has not been included in this book since it will be reported on in depth at a later date[25]. What is appropriate to mention at this point is that it is the nearest thing to a model for evaluating team experiments. First, the experiment and the evaluation have been planned together from the start. Second, because it has made team policing "happen," all of the elements, including geographic stability, have been implemented. Third, it is a model of measurement methods that has maximum chance to yield very firm conclusions on the effects of team policing. The Cincinnati evaluation, being conducted for the Police Foundation by the Urban Institute, includes two kinds of measures. The first kind is a careful monitoring of all relevant data generated by the department in the experimental and control districts: the number and kinds of calls for service, dispatches, reported crimes, complaints, disciplinary actions, sick days, etc. The second, more difficult kind is a series of external measures: surveys of citizen victimization, citizen attitudes about the police, business victimization and businessmen's attitudes, the experiences and attitudes of people who request service from the police, the attitudes and experience of people who are arrested by the police, and the attitudes of both team and non-team police officers toward their job situations and toward their clients. All of these data were gathered as baselines—before the experiment began—and many will be regathered at intervals to measure

[24]DAYTON: Thomas A. Tortoriello and Stephen J. Blatt, *Community Centered Team Policing: A Second Year Evaluation* (Dayton, Ohio: Communication Research Associates, April 1973). DETROIT: Peter B. Bloch and Cyrus Ulberg, "The Beat Commander Concept," *The Police Chief,* September 1972. NEW YORK CITY: Peter B. Bloch and David I. Specht, *Evaluation Report on Operation Neighborhood: A Rapidly Growing Team Policing Program in New York City* (Washington, D. C.: The Urban Institute, Working Paper 4000-3, 1972). SYRACUSE: *Final Report: Crime Control Team II,* OCCP Proposal No. 433, November 1970 to February 1973, prepared for State of New York Office of Crime Control Planning by Syracuse Police Department (Syracuse, N.Y.: 1973). HOLYOKE: *Evaluation Report on the Holyoke Team Police Experiment of the Holyoke Police Department* (Holyoke, Mass.: June 1973).

[25]Evaluation of Cincinnati's Community Sector Team Policing Program, being conducted under contract from the Police Foundation by the Urban Institute.

changes over the life of the experiment. In addition, descriptive accounts of the overall change process in the department constitute a formative component of the research.

Only with considerable effort can the effects of the team policing concept be fully measured. But that does not mean that less grand efforts are wasted. Even the departments that failed to achieve the elements of a team structure seem to have generated many side benefits in the process of change. Not the least of these benefits is the encouragement of discussion about policing concepts that had always been taken for granted. The role of evaluation in such a setting is, again, to say more precisely what happened and why. The important point is that police administrators will have better information for decision-making if independent evaluators are present to give objective feedback.

Evaluations and Decisions

Whenever the first phase of a team policing project ended, the police administrator made a decision about the future of the team project: whether it should be continued, expanded, or discontinued. The effect of the evaluation's findings on that decision was usually quite small, for a number of reasons. First, evaluation often did no more than "prove" what the police administrator already "knew" (intuitively) about team policing, e.g., "the community loves it" or "the other patrolmen hate it." Second, the evaluators themselves often had poor credibility, if not with the police administrator, then with the department. Third, many outside political factors, of necessity, were brought to bear on that "administrative" decision.

Demonstration projects, by definition, proceed from an assumption by the police administrator that the project will work as the way to improve his organization or that it is politically popular and likely to be relatively harmless. In the absence of any persuasive evidence to the contrary, a police administrator is highly likely to feel the same way at the end of the demonstration, regardless of the findings of the evaluation. The decision about what action to take with team policing at the end of the demonstration period, like all highly visible governmental decisions, is political. The factors a chief must consider include opinions of the community, opinions of the political interest groups that support or attack his administration and performance, opinions of the interest groups within the department, and ideally, the most important factor: his judgment as to the effectiveness of the team policing as a means to accomplish certain goals for organizational change. For example, Police Commissioner Nichols in Detroit was presented with clear evidence that the Beat Commander accomplished certain types of organizational changes. His decision not to continue the program was no doubt affected by the police interest groups which opposed a program associated with the internally unpopular administration of former Commissioner Murphy, but that was not the sole consideration. Rather, the disadvantages which had been identified in terms of higher priority departmental goals seemed to have overridden the advantages demonstrated by the evaluation.

Each police department has a different history and different conditions of such resources as leadership, community support, integrity, and initiative. There are problems in all police departments, but those problems vary. There is no one panacea for all of them. Team policing may not be appropriate for many communities even if the Cincinnati results, or results from other cities, are highly favorable. But without good information, there is no way to decide that issue on the facts, and evaluations are necessary to provide that information. Clearly, communities that pay more attention to both the political and the methodological problems of evaluation will get better information about team policing and, thus, be in a position to make sounder decisions concerning the issue.

Chapter VII
Summary and Conclusions

On the basis of the team programs discussed in this report, it would be tempting to conclude that team policing had certain consequences for crime, community relations, and police morale and productivity. The data are far too scant, however, to make such conclusions final. More important is the question many readers will have: should we try team policing in our police department? Most important of all is the question: how can we decide whether team policing makes sense?

Team policing was conceived as a means to an end—a decentralized professional patrol style. In none of the cities studied has that end yet been achieved. The many problems and obstacles experienced by team policing projects merely demonstrate the depth of the change they attempt, which cannot realistically succeed overnight. In all the team policing cities, there were three major reasons that team policing either failed or reached only partial success. These were:

1. Mid-management of the departments, seeing team policing as a threat to their power, subverted and, in some cases, actively sabotaged the plans.

2. The dispatching technology did not permit the patrols to remain in their neighborhoods, despite the stated intentions of adjusting that technology to the pilot projects.

3. The patrols never received a sufficiently clear definition of how

their behavior and role should differ from that of a regular patrol; at the same time, they were considered an elite group by their peers who often resented not having been chosen for the project.

Even if team policing can be implemented as conceived, it is still unclear what effects it may have. To the extent that team policing makes police more responsive to community demands, it might put the police in a crossfire of conflicting goals. On one hand, a decentralized professional model of policing is conceived by many police administrators as a means of making the police "nice guys": polite, observant of citizens' constitutional rights, sensitive to the management of conflict, and honest. On the other hand, the community may make strong demands for the police to be "tough guys" in order to clean up crime, in ways that, if not illegal, are in contradiction to the model conceived by police administrators. For example, data from the evaluation of the New York City program shows that some teams increased the use of aggressive tactics, specifically illegal stop-and-frisks.[26] Early data from the Cincinnati evaluation tentatively suggests the same trend.[27]

There is at present a great concern among police forces and in American cities at large to consider change, to make police officers more responsive to the community. This concern has surfaced in many projects in addition to those labelled "team policing."[28] Whether a specific community should adopt team policing, however, depends first on that community's goals, and second on that community's judgment of team policing's effectiveness within its own situation. Most of all, it depends on both the commitment and the available resources to manage a complex process of institutional and community change.

---

[26]Peter B. Bloch and David I. Specht, *Evaluation Report on Operation Neighborhood* (Washington, D. C.: The Urban Institute, 1972).

[27]Joseph H. Lewis, Director of Evaluation, Police Foundation, personal communication, August 3, 1973.

[28]Efforts to reestablish foot patrol (the pinpoint patrol program in Kansas City) or bicycle patrol (in Baltimore, New York City, and Isla Vista, California) reflect the need on the part of both community and police for more personal contact between the two groups. The Urban Group in the New Orleans Police Department, the Beat Committees in Dallas, and the Pilot District Project in Washington all attempt to improve community relations.